IAN FITZGERALD

ULTIMATE
FOOTBALL HEROES

ACTIVITY
BOOK

DINO

First published by Studio Press Books in 2021,
an imprint of Bonnier Books UK,
The Plaza, 535 King's Road, London SW10 0SZ
Owned by Bonnier Books,
Sveavägen 56, Stockholm, Sweden

www.bonnierbooks.co.uk

Written by Ian Fitzgerald
Designed by Rob Ward
Edited by Saaleh Patel
Production by Nick Read

Paperback ISBN: 978 1 78946 486 3

British Library Cataloguing-in-Publication Data:
A catalogue record for this book is available from the British Library.

Printed and bound in Great Britain by Page Bros Group.

1 3 5 7 9 10 8 6 4 2

To AP. All those hours watching football weren't wasted after all.

TABLE OF CONTENTS

FUN STUFF AND CHALLENGES

Football's a great way to have fun,
whether you're playing the game or enjoying
football-based activities and challenges.

In this section you'll find games, riddles and tons
more to keep you occupied when you're not out
kicking a ball or watching football on the telly.

Have fun and be sure to check the back of the book
for the answers!

THE AMAZING FOOTBALL MAZE

We all want to lift the cup and receive our winners'
medals, but in this challenge you have to find it first.
Be careful, one wrong turn and it's game over!

FOOTBALL JOKES

As someone once said, football's a funny old game, and here's your proof. These football funnies are the best gags we could think of. Do you know any great football-based jokes?

Which team members play best when the pitch is waterlogged?

The subs!

Which Brighton defender, called Lewis, can you dip in your tea?

Lewis Dunk!

Why was Cinderella dropped from the England Lionesses?

She kept running away from the ball!

What did the ref say when the striker was tackled by a chicken?

Fowl!

What do you call it when Robert Lewandowski wears a flat cap, a beanie and a beret, and then makes them disappear?

A hat-trick!

Why did the ref wear two watches to the Champions League final?

He was told that extra time may be needed!

Why is Old Trafford always so windy on match days?

Because it's filled with 76,000 fans!

Why does Lionel Messi wear a bib during games?

Because he's always dribbling!

And here's an old classic... why was Dracula replaced as goalkeeper for the Transylvanian national team?

He was scared of crosses!

BRAINTEASERS

Some of these crafty conundrums might not be what they seem, so try to be creative and think outside the box when you come up with the answers. And pay attention to how the questions are worded.

1 Neymar is so skilful that he can kick the ball fifty metres and make it come straight back and land on his foot. How does he do it?

2 Before the match kicked off, the brainy spectator said the score would be 0–0. And he was correct. How did he know this?

3 What runs around a football pitch but never moves?

4 At an under-11s game, the goalkeeper on the home team has let in four goals in the first thirty minutes.

'You have to take him off at half-time,' the trainer says to the Coach. 'I can't,' says the Coach. 'He's my son. He'll never talk to me again!' But the Coach wasn't the goalkeeper's father. What's going on?

5 Which players in a football team can jump higher than the crossbar?

6 A team played three matches and won one, drew one and lost one. They scored four times and let in four goals, and both teams scored in every game. The game they drew finished 1–1. What were the scores in the other games?

Won:
Drew: 1–1
Lost:

FOOTBALL TRIVIA

When it comes to football, there are lots of stats, facts and figures, but some are more important than others! How much useless stuff do you know about football? Let's find out – circle the correct answers.

1 At size 13½, which player today has the biggest feet in football?

A: Romelu Lukaku   **C:** Virgil van Dijk
B: Zlatan Ibrahimovic

(Fun fact: the biggest boots ever belonged to ex-Arsenal star Kanu, whose feet were a size 15!)

2 Why did Man Utd change out of a grey kit and into a different colour at half-time during a game in 1996 against Southampton?

A: The players claimed they couldn't see each other properly on the pitch.
B: An FA official notified them that it was against the rules at that time to play in grey.
C: They were losing 3–0 and the players said the kit was bringing them bad luck.

3 What was unique about Darren Bent's goal for Sunderland against Liverpool in 2009?

A: The ball bounced off his head while he was knocked out in the penalty area.

B: He ran into the goal with the ball stuffed up his shirt.

C: The ball bounced off an inflatable beach ball a fan had thrown on the pitch.

4 Of all footballers, past and present, who is officially the cleverest?

A: Gerard Piqué
B: Frank Lampard
C: Mario Balotelli

SPOT THE DIFFERENCE

The four footballers here look almost the same, but there are six differences between them. See if you can find them all.

LOST IN TRANSLATION

SPANISH

Una Chilena	Come on ref, blow up
Gol Olimpico	It's hit the post!
Arbitro, la hora	A bicycle kick
Da en el palo	Goal scored directly from a corner

GERMAN

Hexenkessel	It's a six-pointer
Sechspunktespiel	An unfriendly crowd
Fahrstuhlmannschaft	A worldie!
Traumtor	A yo-yo club

Football's a global sport, so it's helpful to know a few handy phrases in other languages. Try matching these common footie terms in Spanish, German, Italian and French to their English versions by drawing a line between them. For each language we've done the first one for you.

ITALIAN

Lui fa un colpo di testa	He's dropped a clanger
Lu fa un Cucchiaio	He's headed the ball
Lui fa una papera	He's nutmegged him!
Lui fa un tunnel	He's scored a 'Panenka' penalty kick

FRENCH

Il est aveugle ou quoi	This ref's rubbish
Une courte victoire	A narrow win
Aux chiottes l'arbitre	Pass it, now!
Passe la balle, nom de dieu	Is the ref blind?

DESIGN YOUR OWN KIT!

Some kits are so cool it seems a shame to get them muddy on a football pitch. Which team's is your favourite? Or maybe it's a combination of kits: Juve's shirt and Barca's shorts. Now you can create your own kit using the drawing below – and colour it in when you're done!

FUNNY FOOTBALL STORIES

**Some – or all – of these funny football stories
are true, and some – or all – of them are false.
Can you guess which is which?
Circle 'TRUE' or 'FALSE' for each story.**

BERNIE'S BARKING MAD

In the 1990 World Cup in Italy, Republic of Ireland
defender Bernie Slaven almost flew home – because
he missed his dogs! While other players phoned
wives and girlfriends every day, Bernie would call his
pampered pooches and bark down the phone at them.

TRUE or FALSE?

SOUTHAMPTON SUCKERED

In 1996, Senegal's Ali Dia asked a friend to call Southampton
manager Graeme Souness and pretend to be FIFA Player of
the Year winner George Weah. On the recommendation of
'Weah', Souness signed Ali Dia, who made his debut days
later as a sub – and was then subbed off again because he
was so terrible! His contract was terminated a few days later.

TRUE or FALSE?

THREE YELLOW CARDS,
ONE RED FACE

English ref Graham Poll embarrassed himself at the 2006 World Cup when, in a game between Croatia and Australia, he issued three yellow cards – to the same player! He booked Croatia's Josip Šimunić in the sixtieth minute, then yellowed him again in the ninetieth, having forgotten he'd already been booked. Then, in the ninety-third minute, Poll gave Šimunić another yellow, followed by a red. It was Poll's last international game.

TRUE or FALSE?

PASSPORTS PLEASE

In 2011, Llansantffraid Village players pranked a teammate when they were due to play fellow Welsh rivals Gwalchmai on the island of Anglesey. Once on the team coach, they asked their fellow player if he'd brought his passport for the trip 'abroad'. He hadn't, of course, and they persuaded him to hide in the coach's luggage compartment as they crossed the 'border'.

TRUE or FALSE?

TAKE THE
STRING CHALLENGE

Only one of the tangled strings below leads to the cup – but which one? Look at the image for ten seconds and decide whether it's A, B or C, then follow your chosen string to see if you were right!

HOME TURF

How well do you know your stadiums? In the left-hand column you will find a list of football clubs and in the right-hand column, a list of stadiums. Match them up with a line. The first one's done for you!

Manchester United	**Anfield**
Leicester City	Santiago Bernabéu
Club América	**Plough Lane**
Arsenal	Fratton Park
Leeds United	**Stadio Renzo Barbera**
Hull City	Stade Louis II
Portsmouth F.C.	**Johan Cruijff ArenA**
Watford F.C.	KCOM Stadium
Liverpool	**San Siro**
Manchester City	Ewood Park
Blackburn Rovers	**Allianz Stadium**
AFC Wimbledon	Emirates Stadium
Borussia Dortmund	**Camp Nou**
A.C. Milan	King Power Stadium
Real Madrid	**Aztec Stadium**
Barcelona	Vicarage Road
Juventus	**Etihad Stadium**
AFC Ajax	Signal Iduna Park
Palermo	**Le Parc des Princes**
AS Monaco	Elland Road
PSG	**Old Trafford**

BEND IT LIKE TRENT

Colour in this flying full-back.

JOIN THE DOTS

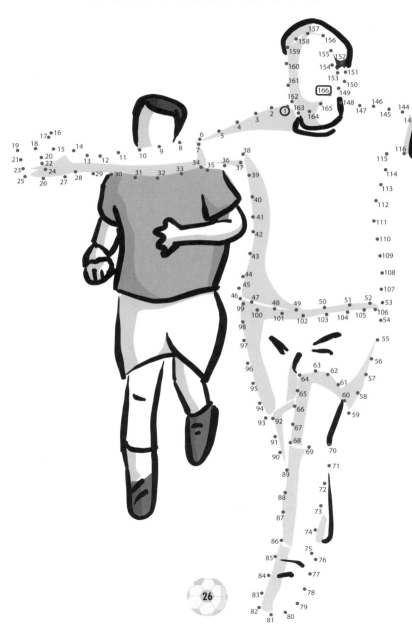

The picture here may look like a bit of a mess, but join the dots carefully and a football-based picture should soon become clear. Once you've finished, why not colour it in, too?

WORLD CUP HEROES

Here's a great way to remember the eleven English legends that won the World Cup in 1966.
Grab a pen and a piece of paper, study the word map below for thirty seconds, then cover it up and write down as many of the names as you can remember.

BOBBY MOORE
ROGER HUNT
GEORGE COHEN
GORDON
Ray Wilson
BANKS
MARTIN PETERS
Nobby Stiles
ALAN BALL
Jack Charlton
GEOFF HURST
BOBBY CHARLTON

WRITE A FAN LETTER

Have you ever dreamed of writing a fan letter to your favourite player? Now's your chance! Ask them anything you want, and tell them why you think they're such a great footballer. Maybe it's their skill, their passion or their sheer will to win that inspires you!

DRAWING GRID
CHALLENGE

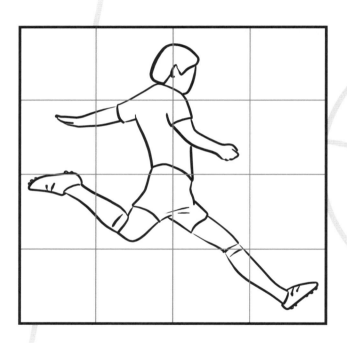

Want to learn to draw this super striker?

Copy the image on the left, square by square,
into the grid on the right and you'll eventually
see that you've made a perfect replica!

MINDFULNESS EXERCISE

Completing a simple task is a great way to calm your mind and make you feel happy and relaxed. It's what experts call 'mindfulness', and it's something we all need to do now and then.

Colouring-in is the perfect mindfulness exercise:
it's easy but it's also creative and really satisfying.

Take your time colouring in the image below – not just
the jumping figures, but the flags, the mobiles phones and
the hats. Then take note of how you feel afterwards!

BE A FOOTBALL COMMENTATOR!

1   Prepare, prepare, prepare. Pick an upcoming game that's being shown on TV and read, write down and remember as many facts, figures and stats about the players and teams as you can.

2   Get your voice right. Football commentators don't sound the same as 'normal' people. Listen to them on the radio or TV and notice how they use their voice, when they speed up and slow down, for example, or when they get excited.

3   Don't show off. You'll have all your stats to hand, but don't just reel off lists and lists of all the info. Drop in little facts and bits of information now and then. Less is more.

It's a dream job, right?
You go to games for free, have the best seat in the
house and you get to interview the players afterwards.
But being a football commentator's not as easy as
it sounds, so here's our advice on how to do it.

4 Keep talking. Sometimes, there's nothing much
happening in a game – but that doesn't mean you
stay silent. Quite the opposite, in fact! The more
uneventful the game, the more you have to speak,
so have a few stories ready to tell, just in case.

5 Go to the loo
before kick-off!

6 Okay, ready? Right, when the game
you've chosen is on TV, turn down
the volume, wait for the ref to
start the game... and go for it!

THE HURRIKANE

Colour in this
superstar striker.

FOOTBALL SNAKES AND LADDERS

Football's a game of ups and downs, and that's why we've created this fun game of football snakes and ladders. You can play on your own, or with friends and family, all you need is a die and some counters.

FULL TIME	RED CARD Bye-bye!	33	32	31	30
24	25	26	27	28	29
23	22	21	Miss a penalty!	19	2–0 up at half-time!
OWN GOAL! Oh nooo…	13	NUTMEG a defender!	15	16	17
11	10	9	8	7	6
KICK OFF	You make a goal-line clearance!	2	3	4	5

CREATE A "FLIP BOOK" CARTOON

Making a 'flip book' cartoon is really easy and it will look amazing. Follow the steps below and draw or trace the images in the top-right corner of each page of a spare scrapbook. When you've drawn them all, flip through the pages of the book and watch your cartoon come to life. Magic!

PLAY
FOOTBALL BINGO

HE'S LOST THE DRESSING ROOM	WHAT'S THE REF GIVEN HERE	I'VE SEEN THEM GIVEN	IT'S A GAME OF TWO HALVES
2–0'S A DANGEROUS LEAD	THEY'VE PARKED THE BUS	THE COMMENTATOR'S CURSE	THIS GAME NEEDS A GOAL
HE'S GOT TO HIT THE TARGET FROM THERE!	HE'LL BE SICK AS A PARROT	THEY'LL BE OVER THE MOON	ON PAPER THEY ARE THE BETTER SIDE
I FANCY THEM IN THE CUP THIS YEAR	A CRUNCHING TACKLE!	AT THE END OF THE DAY	IT'S A SIX-POINTER

Next time you're watching a football match on the telly, play this game along with it. Whenever you hear a commentator use one of the footie phrases below, cross it off the bingo card. We've made two cards, so you can play against a friend. First one to fill up their card wins!

IF THAT'S ON TARGET, IT GOES IN	IT'S A SIX-POINTER	SOME TIRED LEGS OUT THERE	WHERE WAS THE MARKING?
THEY'LL BE OVER THE MOON	HE'LL BE GUTTED ABOUT THAT	I FANCY THEM IN THE CUP THIS YEAR	A GOOD TIME TO SCORE
NO EASY GAMES AT THIS LEVEL	HE'S LOST THE DRESSING ROOM	HE'S A NO-NONSENSE PLAYER	GOOD TOUCH FOR A BIG MAN
SCHOOLBOY DEFENDING	THEY'VE PARKED THE BUS	HE'S GOT TO SCORE THAT	HONOURS EVEN

BUILD THE PERFECT PLAYER

Imagine a footballer with Ronaldo's heading ability, Messi's dribbling, Megan Rapinoe's will to win, and David Beckham's dead-ball skills! In this challenge, you're going to build your own perfect player! List your favourite player for each of the skills below, then finish off the drawing.

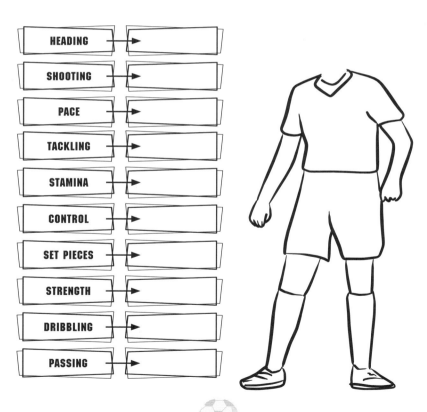

HEADING	→
SHOOTING	→
PACE	→
TACKLING	→
STAMINA	→
CONTROL	→
SET PIECES	→
STRENGTH	→
DRIBBLING	→
PASSING	→

PORTUGUESE MAGNIFICO

Colour in this midfield maestro.

PIN THE INJURY ON THE PLAYER!

Players are always 'doing their hamstring' or 'tweaking an Achilles' – but where are these mysterious body parts?

Match each injury to the spot where it belongs on our injury-prone player.

(1) Dislocated glenoid

(2) Pulled hamstring

(3) Damaged Achilles

(4) Fractured clavicle

(5) Concussion

(6) Quadriceps strain

(7) Anterior cruciate ligament [ACL] injury

(8) Shin splints

(9) Sprained impingement

(10) Broken metatarsal

(11) Groin pull

DO THE ROBOT!

3 June 2006 is a day that will live in football history.

Yes, it was the first time that Peter Crouch did the now-legendary robot dance (when he scored for England against Jamaica).

Since then, many people have tried to copy the lanky striker's awesome moves, but few have succeeded.

Now it's your turn!

Follow the steps below and learn how to do the robot!

STEP 1

Lean forwards a little, lock both elbows at right angles, like you're holding a parcel, then raise your left arm, keeping it locked.

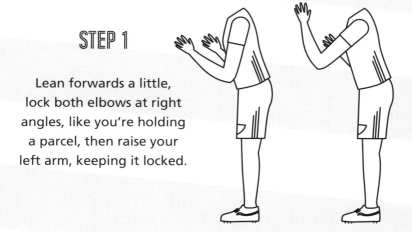

Straighten up your back, and, keeping your arms locked, pump them up and down (as though you are running), but in a slow-motion and jerky way. As you do this slowly turn your body to the left, then to the right.

Now lean backwards a little, keep pumping your arms and turning from left to right.

Once you've got these basic moves, start to freestyle – maybe throw in a moonwalk!

JACK
THE LADS

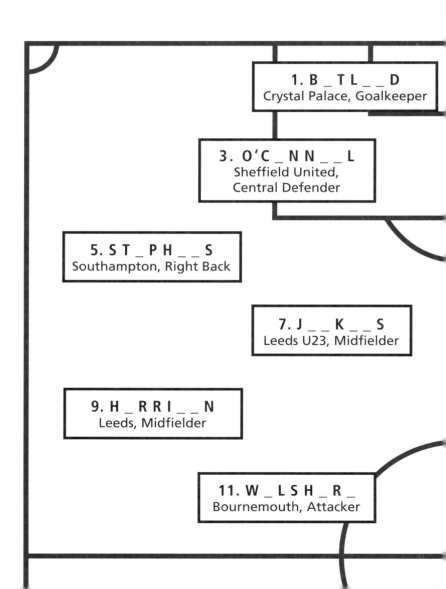

1. B _ T L _ _ D
Crystal Palace, Goalkeeper

3. O'C _ N N _ _ L
Sheffield United,
Central Defender

5. S T _ P H _ _ S
Southampton, Right Back

7. J _ _ K _ _ S
Leeds U23, Midfielder

9. H _ R R I _ _ N
Leeds, Midfielder

11. W _ L S H _ R _
Bournemouth, Attacker

Have you noticed how every other player is called 'Jack' these days? Every team seems to have at least one. See if you can fill in the blanks and complete this line-up of famous Jacks, old and new. (We've put their most recent clubs next to their names to help you out.)

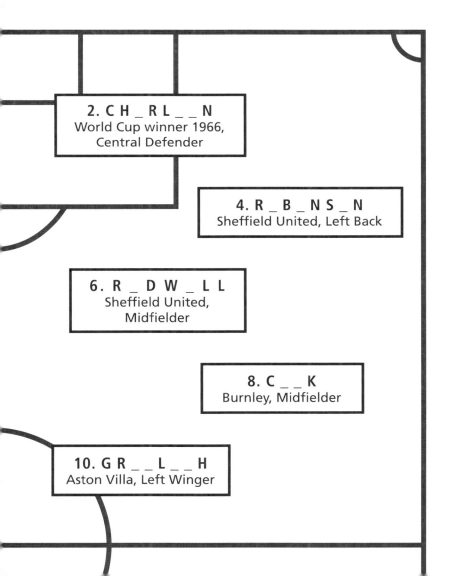

2. C H _ R L _ _ N
World Cup winner 1966,
Central Defender

4. R _ B _ N S _ N
Sheffield United, Left Back

6. R _ D W _ L L
Sheffield United,
Midfielder

8. C _ _ K
Burnley, Midfielder

10. G R _ _ L _ _ H
Aston Villa, Left Winger

KING OF EUROPE

Colour in this
goal-scoring machine.

WHERE IN THE WORLD?

How's your geography? In the next few pages we'll ask you to locate places that are home to some famous (and not so famous) football teams. Don't worry, we've given you clues to help you find them all!

Remember, you can look for these places on a real map, too. After all, geography's not just about knowing where places are, it's also about hunting for places on maps!

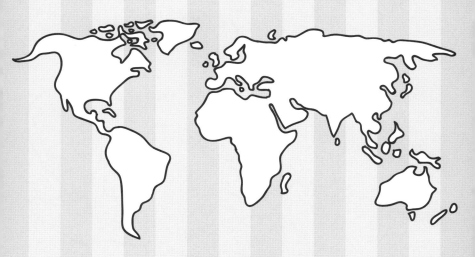

A:

B:

C:

D:

E:

F:

WHERE IN THE WORLD?
UNITED KINGDOM

How well do you know the locations of the UK's football teams? On the map opposite we've pinned some towns and cities that are home to some well-known football teams. Follow the clues below and write your answers in the boxes opposite.

1. England's capital on the River Thames and home to more than a dozen league clubs, including Arsenal, West Ham, Brentford, QPR and Leyton Orient.

2. Celtic and Rangers are the two big teams in this Scottish city on the River Clyde.

3. The Red Devils are based in this rainy city.

4. Norwich City's great local rivals, known as the Tractor Boys.

5. The Magpies are based in this 'Toon' on the River Tyne in the northeast.

6. South Wales city and club. Also home to the country's national rugby stadium.

WHERE IN THE WORLD?
FRANCE

France is known for its world-class footballers. Platini, Henry and Mbappé all began their careers on home soil, playing for French clubs. But do you know where those clubs are?

1. It's what the 'P' in PSG stands for and it's the capital of France, where you can climb the Eiffel Tower.

2. It's where Kylian Mbappé began his career. It's an anagram of ACONOM and technically it's not part of France!

3. This town's team in the north of France is called Racing Club de _ _ _ _. (Clue: if you don't want to wear glasses you can wear a contact _ _ _ _.)

4. This club and town in eastern France is also the name of a type of mustard. It's an anagram of JODIN.

5. This city is found on the south coast of France. Ex-players include Didier Drogba, Eric Cantona and Joey Barton! Careful, it's hard to spell: M_R_E_L_E.

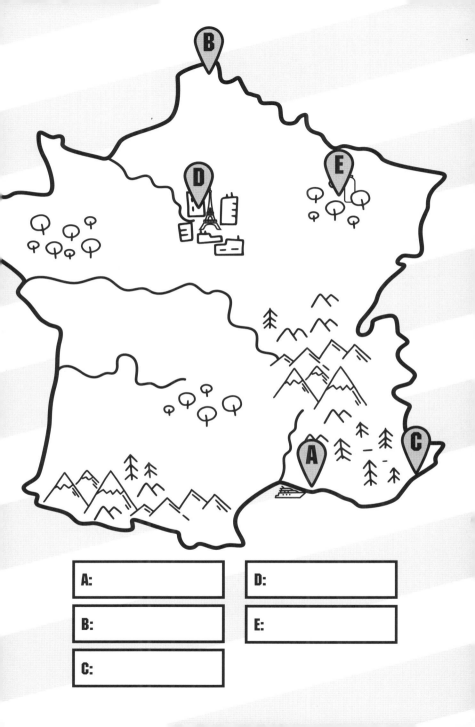

A:	D:
B:	E:
C:	

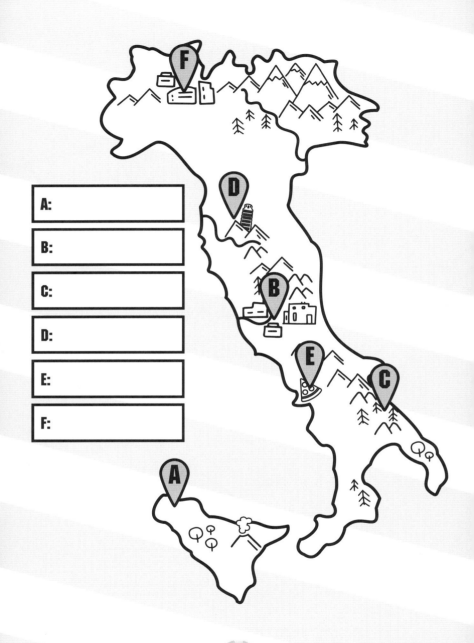

A:

B:

C:

D:

E:

F:

WHERE IN THE WORLD?
ITALY

In Italy they call football *Calcio!* Look at the map and try to solve the clues to reveal some of Italy's most beautiful cities. *Buona fortuna* (and give yourself a bonus point if you can work out what that means).

1. Yum! They say pizza was invented in this southern Italian city, whose team is called Napoli.

2. Italy's capital city on the River Tiber and where Roma and Lazio play. The Colosseum's there, too.

3. Inter _ _ _ _ _ and A.C. _ _ _ _ _ are based in northern Italy's fashion capital near the Alps.

4. The capital of Sicily, its football club has the same name as the city: P_L_R_O. It's also close to a massive volcano.

5. Italy looks like a high-heeled boot, doesn't it? This city at the top of the heel is an anagram of ABRI.

6. This city has a football club and a leaning tower!

WHERE IN THE WORLD? SPAIN AND PORTUGAL

These two countries have some incredible football clubs whose histories are as amazing as the cities they call home – all you've got to do is identify them.

1. Messi. Say no more. It's up in the northeast of Spain.

2. Zidane played for 'Real' in this city, so did Beckham, Bale, Ronaldo… it's Spain's capital, too.

3. Sporting L_ _ _ _ N are based in Portugal's capital, where Benfica play.

4. They call this city and football club 'Sevilla' in Spain, but the English version is different by just one letter.

5. This city (and club) in northern Portugal is where players like Pepe and Deco made their names. It's an anagram of TROOP.

6. You may have been on holiday to the seaside town of M_L_G_ on Spain's Costa del Sol. Ex-players include Santi Cazorla and Isco.

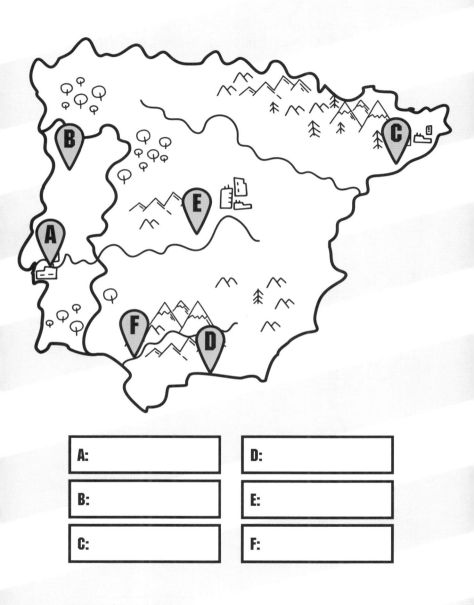

A:	D:
B:	E:
C:	F:

A:	D:
B:	E:
C:	F:

WHERE IN THE WORLD?
GERMANY

Germany is a true footballing powerhouse. So it's time to find out where all those successful football clubs and players come from. Solve the clues and name the cities on the map opposite.

1. Bayern M_ _ _ _ H. Lewandowski. What else is there to say?

2. Borussia M_ N _H _ N _ L _ D _A _H. This city is in the west of the country, close to the border with the Netherlands.

3. This German city is home to Eintracht F_ _ _ _ _ _ _T. The citizens of this city also sound a bit like sausages!

4. People from this city sound like something you'd put in a bun with ketchup. Yum!

5. Hertha _ _ _ _ _ _ play in the German capital. It's home to a famous Wall, the Brandenburg Gate and the TV Tower, the country's tallest building.

6. The home town of Werder B_ _ _ _ N, up on Germany's chilly north coast.

WHERE IN THE WORLD?
USA

Yes, we know, they call it 'soccer', but that's fine, they'll get the hang of calling it footie one day. As football becomes more popular in the US of A, let's find out where they play the game.

1. D.C. United play here, in America's capital – which is named after their first president George W _ _ _ _ _ _ _ N.

2. The Big Apple. America's most populous city and home to a football club of the same name.

3. West coast city whose name in English is 'The Angels' and where you'll find Hollywood and LA Galaxy.

4. 'H _ _ _ _ _N, we have a problem!' This Texas city's football club are known as the Dynamos.

5. Inter M _ _ _ I. Part-owned by David Beckham.

6. This city in the US state of Tennessee is famous for its country and western music: N_S_V_L_E.

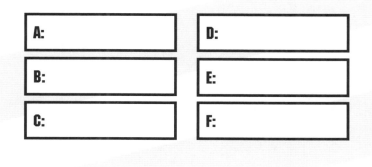

A:

B:

C:

D:

E:

F:

A:

B:

C:

D:

E:

F:

WHERE IN THE WORLD?
SOUTH AMERICA

South America has produced some of the greatest players ever: Messi, Maradona, Pelé, Suárez. But do you know where most of these players learned their craft? Let's find out!

1. Diego Maradona's old club Boca Juniors is in this city, the capital of Argentina. Its name in English means 'Fair winds' or 'good air', but in Spanish it's B_E_O_ / A_R_S.

2. Corinthians, one of Brazil's biggest clubs, comes from this city. Its English name is 'Saint Paul' (in Brazil, it's S_O / P_ U _O).

3. Brazilian club Flamengo play at the famous Maracanã Stadium in this city, R_O / D_ / J_ N_I_ O. The Copacabana Beach is here.

4. Colombia's capital city, an anagram of TOBAGO (B_ _ _ _ Á), is home to the clubs La Equidad and Santa Fe.

5. The highest stadium in the world is home to Peru's Unión Minas, at 13,973 ft! It's in the Andes Mountains.

WHERE IN THE WORLD?
AFRICA

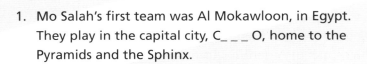

African footballers play for some of the world's biggest clubs, but what about football teams in Africa? See if you can match up the clues to their location on the map. Use an atlas if you want!

1. Mo Salah's first team was Al Mokawloon, in Egypt. They play in the capital city, C_ _ _ O, home to the Pyramids and the Sphinx.

2. Tusker F.C. is a Kenyan team based in the country's capital N_ _ _ _ _ I. The club badge is an elephant holding a football in its trunk!

3. Zimbabwe's Gunners F.C. play in an Arsenal-style kit even though they're located on the capital city of H_R_R_.

4. You'll find this South African coastal city and club at the south-western tip of the country, with Table Mountain in the background. It's an anagram of PACE / NOWT.

5. A.S. Dragons are one of the top teams of the Democratic Republic of the Congo. They play in the capital city of K_N_H_S_.

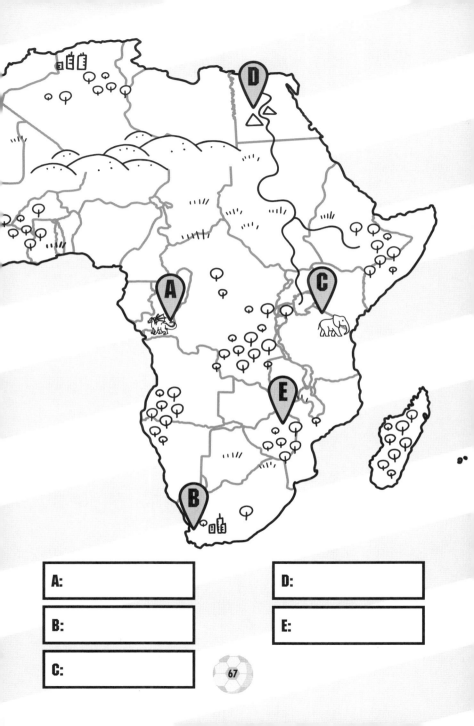

A:

B:

C:

D:

E:

YOU'RE THE REF

This is your chance to be a referee! Think of the power, the responsibility and the cool gadgets in the age of VAR (video assistant referee). In the next few pages you'll get to decide what to do in some weird, wonderful, funny and controversial situations.

Ready? Okay, let's kick off.

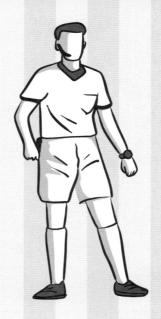

1 A player scores then takes his top off to celebrate. Before you have the chance to caution him (as the rules tell you to) VAR tells you the goal is offside.
What do you do?

A: Tell the player to put his top on and restart play

B: Yellow card the player and restart play

C: Yellow card the player and allow the goal

2 A keeper saves a penalty. But VAR tells you they were standing behind the line when the ball was kicked.
What do you do?

A: Nothing. The keeper saved it. Play on

B: Award a goal – if the keeper saved the ball behind the line

C: Make the player retake the penalty

3 During play, the fourth official (VAR) tells you someone on one of the benches has done something worthy of a yellow or red card – but he doesn't know who. What do you do?

A: Tell the bench to calm down and let them off with a warning

B: Pick a member of the bench at random and yellow or red card them

C: Yellow or red card the manager/head coach

4 An outfield player punches the ball off the line to prevent a goal. Do you...

A: Give the player a yellow card

B: Red card the player and award a penalty

C: Yellow card the player and award a penalty

5   The keeper catches the ball and accidentally runs out of their penalty area and into the 'D', still holding the ball. What's your decision?

A: Blow for a drop ball

B: Award a penalty

C: Give a direct free kick

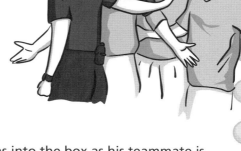

6   A player runs into the box as his teammate is taking a penalty – which the keeper saves. Sort that one out, ref!

A: Retake the penalty

B: Indirect free kick to the defending team

C: Goal kick to the defending team

7 At a dropped ball, a player kicks the ball straight into the net. How do you restart the game?

A: Goal kick (i.e. disallow the goal)

B: Kick-off (i.e. allow the goal)

C: Direct free kick for the defending team at the drop ball position

8 A defender accidentally fouls a player in his penalty box. How do you penalise him?

A: Give a penalty and send him off

B: Give a direct free kick

C: Give a penalty with no card

9 In a bad-tempered game, you've sent off three players from each team. How many more players from either team can you dismiss before you must abandon the game.

A: One

B: Two

C: Three

10 The keeper handles the ball in the area from a back-pass by a teammate. This offence is worthy of a…

A: Direct free kick

B: Indirect free kick

C: Penalty

11 An attacking player taking a throw-in throws the ball to a teammate in an offside position, who goes on to score. Do you…

A: Allow the goal

B: Order the throw-in to be retaken

C: Award a goal kick (i.e. disallow the goal)

12 A sub is waiting to come on when the ball goes out of play next to him. The player he's replacing has been carried off injured on the other side of the pitch, so can the incoming player take the throw-in?

A: Yes

B: No

13 An attacking team takes a corner, but as the ball is kicked the wind catches it and the ball flies up the other end of the pitch and goes straight into the attacking team's goal. What do you award?

A: Corner kick to the defending team

B: Goal kick to the attacking team

C: Allow the goal

14 One player deliberately knocks out an opponent. Which of the following actions are you not permitted to take?

A: Book or send off the offending player

B: Stop the clock until play is ready to resume

C: Personally provide medical treatment for the injured player

15 It's 0–0 with seconds to go in a game. You decide to blow for time, but as you put the whistle to your lips you stumble and it falls into the mud at your feet. In the meantime, one team scores a goal. Do you let the goal stand?

A: Yes, you hadn't blown the whistle

B: No, the goal was scored after you intended to blow the whistle

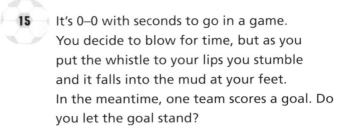

16 A player takes a throw-in and it goes straight into the goal without anyone else touching it. Do you…

A: Allow the goal

B: Give a goal kick to the defending team

C: Give a corner kick to the attacking team

FANTASY FOOTBALL

Putting a football team together isn't easy, even if you've got £300 million to spend – as you're about to find out! It's time to play fantasy football.

All you have to do is assemble some teams from the greatest players ever – and match them up against each other.

MEN'S DREAM TEAM

For this challenge you've got £300 million to spend on a team. You're going to create a super XI using the list of players below.

GOALKEEPERS

GORDON BANKS **8**   PETER SCHMEICHEL **8**   IKER CASILLAS **10**

LEV YASHIN **10**   MANUEL NEUER **12**   GIANLUIGI BUFFON **12**

CENTRE-BACKS

ALDAIR **12**   JOHN TERRY **12**   CLAUDIO GENTILE **14**   TONY ADAMS **14**

LAURENT BLANC **15**   RIO FERDINAND **16**   GIORGIO CHIELLINI **18**   BOBBY MOORE **18**

CARLOS PUYOL **20**   RONALD KOEMAN **22**   FRANCO BARESI **24**   FABIO CANNAVARO **25**

SERGIO RAMOS **25**   VIRGIL VAN DIJK **27**   FRANZ BECKENBAUER **28**

MIDFIELDERS

MASON MOUNT **20**   PHIL FODEN **20**   PAUL POGBA **25**   JAMES RODRIGUEZ **25**

BRUNO FERNANDES **28**   JORDAN HENDERSON **28**   PATRICK VIERA **30**   N'GOLO KANTÉ **30**

ROY KEANE **33**   CESC FABREGAS **33**   PAUL SCHOLES **35**   STEVEN GERRARD **37**

YAYA TOURÉ **39**   PAUL GASCOIGNE **42**   ANDREA PIRLO **45**   MICHEL PLATINI **46**

KEVIN DE BRUYNE **48**   ANDRÉS INIESTA **50**   XAVI **52**   ZINEDINE ZIDANE **55**

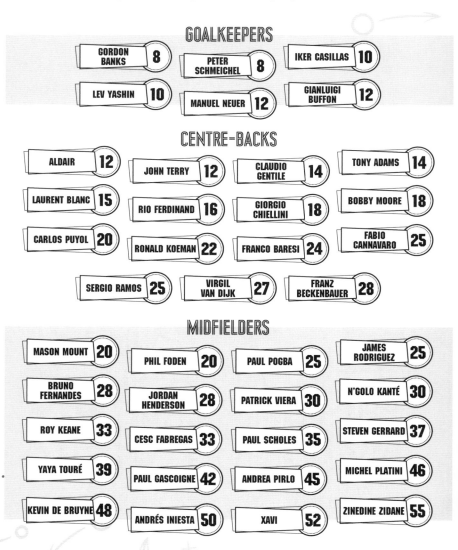

Think about it carefully and choose the players you think would make the best team. Don't just go for modern-day players. Look up the videos and stats of some of the players you don't know – you'll be amazed how good they were!

Turn the page and write your choices in the correct positions to complete your dream team.

(The number next to each player is their value in £ millions.)

FULL-BACKS

JAVIER ZANETTI	8
JOÃO CANCELO	8
PHILIPP LAHM	10
KYLE WALKER	10
ASHLEY COLE	12
BIXENTE LIZARAZU	14
DANI ALVES	14
ROBERTO CARLOS	16
TRENT ALEXANDER ARNOLD	18
ANDREW ROBERTSON	18

WINGERS / WIDE PLAYERS

SERGE GNABRY	18
JACK GREALISH	18
RIYAD MAHREZ	20
JOHN BARNES	22
RAHEEM STERLING	23
MOHAMED SALAH	26
DAVID BECKHAM	28
ARJEN ROBBEN	30
LUÍS FIGO	33
EDEN HAZARD	35
GEORGE BEST	36
RYAN GIGGS	36
GARETH BALE	38
JOHAN CRUYFF	40
RONALDINHO	40
CRISTIANO RONALDO	60

FORWARDS

HARRY KANE	40
ALFREDO DI STÉFANO	42
DIDIER DROGBA	43
LUIS SUÁREZ	44
ALAN SHEARER	46
MARCO VAN BASTEN	48
ZLATAN IBRAHIMOVIC	50
IAN RUSH	50
NEYMAR	52
WAYNE ROONEY	52
RONALDO	54
ROBERT LEWANDOWSKI	56
THIERRY HENRY	58
GERD MÜLLER	58
PELÉ	60
LIONEL MESSI	63
DIEGO MARADONA	65

MEN'S DREAM TEAM

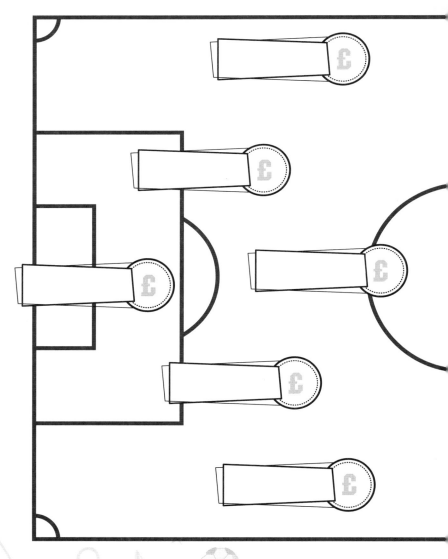

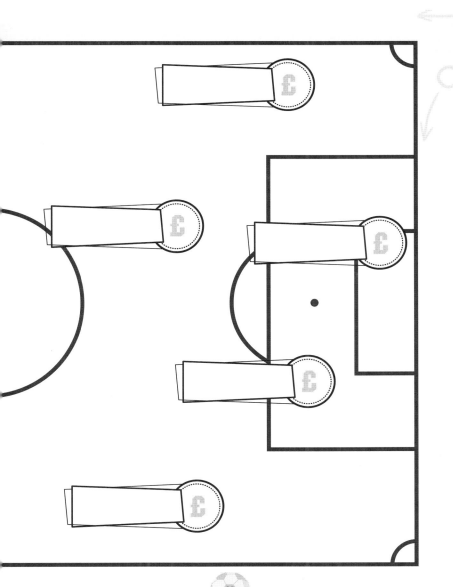

81

WOMEN'S DREAM TEAM

If you know women's football,
great – because it's awesome! If you
don't, now's the time to find out about it.

GOALKEEPERS

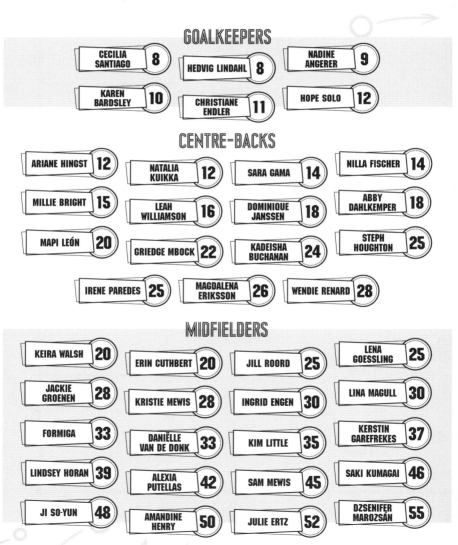

CECILIA SANTIAGO 8	HEDVIG LINDAHL 8	NADINE ANGERER 9
KAREN BARDSLEY 10	CHRISTIANE ENDLER 11	HOPE SOLO 12

CENTRE-BACKS

ARIANE HINGST 12	NATALIA KUIKKA 12	SARA GAMA 14	NILLA FISCHER 14
MILLIE BRIGHT 15	LEAH WILLIAMSON 16	DOMINIQUE JANSSEN 18	ABBY DAHLKEMPER 18
MAPI LEÓN 20	GRIEDGE MBOCK 22	KADEISHA BUCHANAN 24	STEPH HOUGHTON 25
IRENE PAREDES 25	MAGDALENA ERIKSSON 26	WENDIE RENARD 28	

MIDFIELDERS

KEIRA WALSH 20	ERIN CUTHBERT 20	JILL ROORD 25	LENA GOESSLING 25
JACKIE GROENEN 28	KRISTIE MEWIS 28	INGRID ENGEN 30	LINA MAGULL 30
FORMIGA 33	DANIËLLE VAN DE DONK 33	KIM LITTLE 35	KERSTIN GAREFREKES 37
LINDSEY HORAN 39	ALEXIA PUTELLAS 42	SAM MEWIS 45	SAKI KUMAGAI 46
JI SO-YUN 48	AMANDINE HENRY 50	JULIE ERTZ 52	DZSENIFER MAROZSÁN 55

You know the drill: you have £300 million to spend on a team. Think about who you'd like for your team and pick the best players (within budget!) to fit.

Turn the page to fill in your dream team.

(The number next to each player is their value in £ millions.)

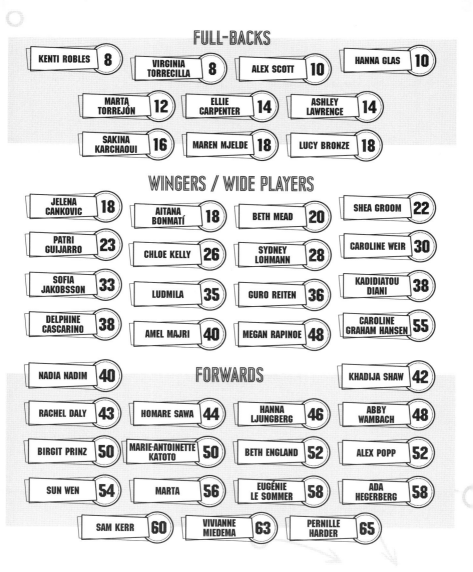

FULL-BACKS

KENTI ROBLES 8 — VIRGINIA TORRECILLA 8 — ALEX SCOTT 10 — HANNA GLAS 10

MARTA TORREJÓN 12 — ELLIE CARPENTER 14 — ASHLEY LAWRENCE 14

SAKINA KARCHAOUI 16 — MAREN MJELDE 18 — LUCY BRONZE 18

WINGERS / WIDE PLAYERS

JELENA CANKOVIC 18 — AITANA BONMATÍ 18 — BETH MEAD 20 — SHEA GROOM 22

PATRI GUIJARRO 23 — CHLOE KELLY 26 — SYDNEY LOHMANN 28 — CAROLINE WEIR 30

SOFIA JAKOBSSON 33 — LUDMILA 35 — GURO REITEN 36 — KADIDIATOU DIANI 38

DELPHINE CASCARINO 38 — AMEL MAJRI 40 — MEGAN RAPINOE 48 — CAROLINE GRAHAM HANSEN 55

FORWARDS

NADIA NADIM 40 — KHADIJA SHAW 42

RACHEL DALY 43 — HOMARE SAWA 44 — HANNA LJUNGBERG 46 — ABBY WAMBACH 48

BIRGIT PRINZ 50 — MARIE-ANTOINETTE KATOTO 50 — BETH ENGLAND 52 — ALEX POPP 52

SUN WEN 54 — MARTA 56 — EUGÉNIE LE SOMMER 58 — ADA HEGERBERG 58

SAM KERR 60 — VIVIANNE MIEDEMA 63 — PERNILLE HARDER 65

WOMEN'S DREAM TEAM

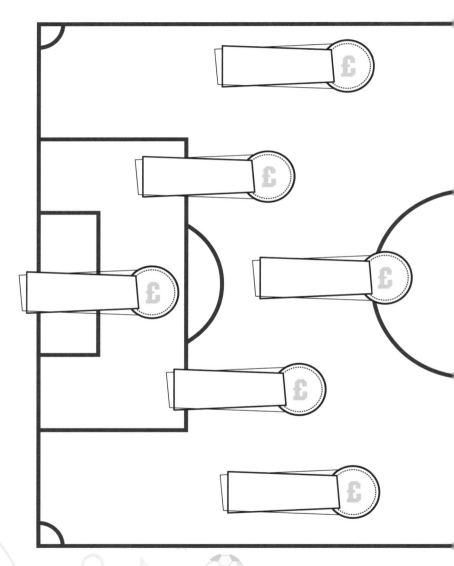

Complete your dream team and
then add up the total value.

TOTAL

_____ /300 MILLION

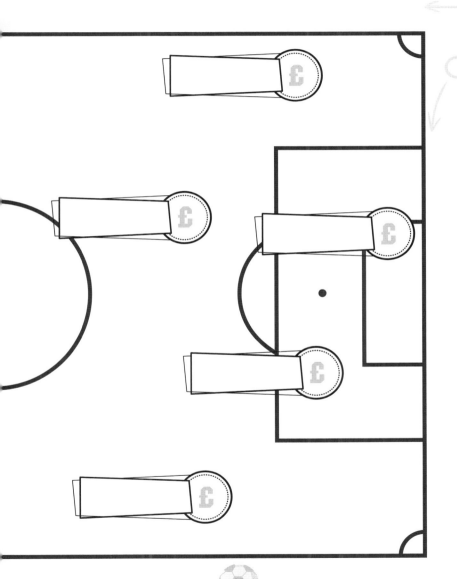

ULTIMATE ENGLAND V GERMANY MEN'S TEAMS

ENGLAND

GOALKEEPERS

GORDON BANKS	JOE HART	PETER SHILTON	DAVID SEAMAN

FULL BACKS

ASHLEY COLE	TRENT ALEXANDER-ARNOLD	STUART PEARCE
KYLE WALKER	GRAEME LE SAUX	GARY NEVILLE

CENTRE-BACKS

GARETH SOUTHGATE	BOBBY MOORE	TONY ADAMS
JOHN TERRY	RIO FERDINAND	JACK CHARLTON

WINGERS/WIDE PLAYERS

JACK GREALISH	JOHN BARNES	CHRIS WADDLE
STEVE MCMANAMAN	STANLEY MATTHEWS	DAVID BECKHAM

MIDFIELDERS

GLENN HODDLE	PAUL GASCOIGNE	NOBBY STILES	FRANK LAMPARD
ALAN BALL	BOBBY CHARLTON	STEVEN GERRARD	JORDAN HENDERSON

FORWARDS

HARRY KANE	KEVIN KEEGAN	ALAN SHEARER	WAYNE ROONEY
GARY LINEKER	GEOFF HURST	MARCUS RASHFORD	JIMMY GREAVES

Okay, this is the big one. You've got two lists: some of the best English and German players of all time and all you have to do is pick the best XI v XI. No budget to worry about this time. Game on!

Turn the page to complete your dream line-ups.

GERMANY

GOALKEEPERS

MANUEL NEUER	OLIVER KAHN	MARC-ANDRÉ TER STEGEN	SEPP MAIER

FULL BACKS

PHILIPP LAHM	PAUL BREITNER	BERTI VOGTS
ANDREAS BREHME	JOSHUA KIMMICH	THOMAS BERTHOLD

CENTRE-BACKS

FRANZ BECKENBAUER	ANTONIO RÜDIGER	MATS HUMMELS
JÉRÔME BOATENG	MATTHIAS SAMMER	KLAUS AUGENTHALER

WINGERS/WIDE PLAYERS

PIERRE LITTBARSKI	SERGE GNABRY	HELMUT RAHN
LEROY SANÉ	WOLFGANG OVERATH	LUKAS PODOLSKI

MIDFIELDERS

LOTHAR MATTHÄUS	TONI KROOS	THOMAS MÜLLER	ÍLKAY GÜNDOGAN
MICHAEL BALLACK	ANDREAS MÖLLER	MESUT ÖZIL	BASTIAN SCHWEINSTEIGER

FORWARDS

GERD MÜLLER	JÜRGEN KLINSMANN	MIROSLAV KLOSE	MARCO REUS
RUDI VÖLLER	KARL-HEINZ RUMMENIGGE	TIMO WERNER	OLIVER BIERHOFF

ULTIMATE ENGLAND V GERMANY

ENGLAND

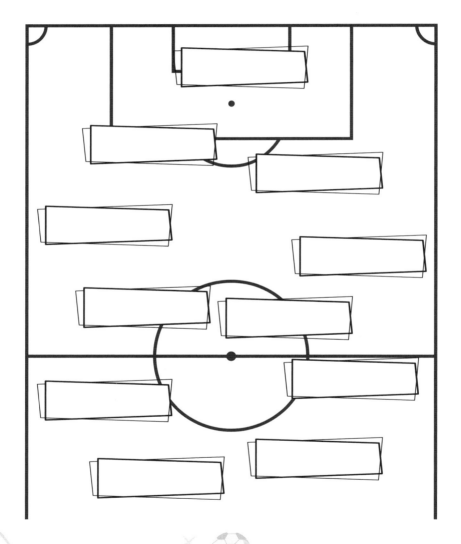

Fill in your ultimate men's XI for England and Germany.

GERMANY

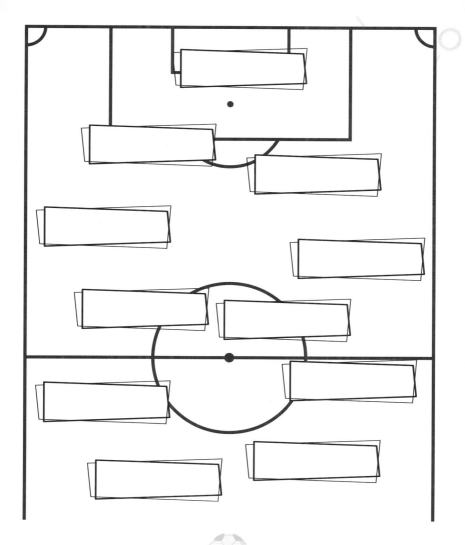

ULTIMATE ENGLAND V USA WOMEN'S TEAMS

ENGLAND

GOALKEEPERS

ELLIE ROEBUCK	KAREN BARDSLEY	SANDY MACIVER	CARLY TELFORD

FULL BACKS

LUCY BRONZE	RACHEL DALY	ALEX SCOTT
ALEX GREENWOOD	MICHELLE HICKMOTT	CLAIRE RAFFERTY

CENTRE-BACKS

STEPH HOUGHTON	ANITA ASANTE	LINDSAY JOHNSON
LEAH WILLIAMSON	JEMMA ROSE	CASEY STONEY

WINGERS/WIDE PLAYERS

JILL SCOTT	KAREN CARNEY	RACHEL YANKEY
SUE SMITH	TONI DUGGAN	JODY HANDLEY

MIDFIELDERS

DEBBIE BAMPTON	MILLIE BRIGHT	CARLY HUNT
FARA WILLIAMS	JORDAN NOBBS	HOPE POWELL

FORWARDS

FRAN KIRBY	KELLY SMITH	ENI ALUKO
BETH ENGLAND	NIKITA PARRIS	BETH MEAD

America has dominated women's football recently, but England's Lionesses are coming through as their main rivals. Let's create an ultimate England XI and pit them against the USA's strongest line up. What a match that would be!

Turn the page to complete your dream line-ups.

USA

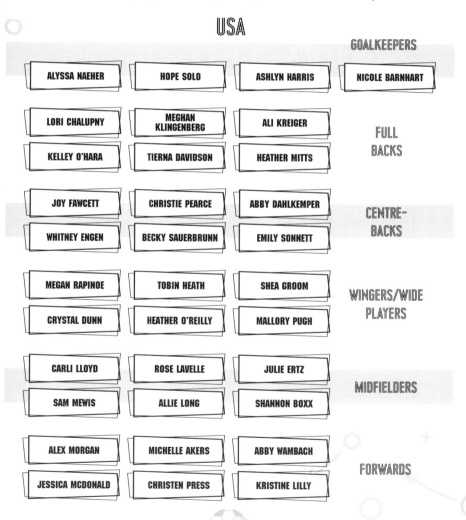

GOALKEEPERS

ALYSSA NAEHER	HOPE SOLO	ASHLYN HARRIS	NICOLE BARNHART

FULL BACKS

LORI CHALUPNY	MEGHAN KLINGENBERG	ALI KREIGER
KELLEY O'HARA	TIERNA DAVIDSON	HEATHER MITTS

CENTRE-BACKS

JOY FAWCETT	CHRISTIE PEARCE	ABBY DAHLKEMPER
WHITNEY ENGEN	BECKY SAUERBRUNN	EMILY SONNETT

WINGERS/WIDE PLAYERS

MEGAN RAPINOE	TOBIN HEATH	SHEA GROOM
CRYSTAL DUNN	HEATHER O'REILLY	MALLORY PUGH

MIDFIELDERS

CARLI LLOYD	ROSE LAVELLE	JULIE ERTZ
SAM MEWIS	ALLIE LONG	SHANNON BOXX

FORWARDS

ALEX MORGAN	MICHELLE AKERS	ABBY WAMBACH
JESSICA MCDONALD	CHRISTEN PRESS	KRISTINE LILLY

ULTIMATE ENGLAND V USA

ENGLAND

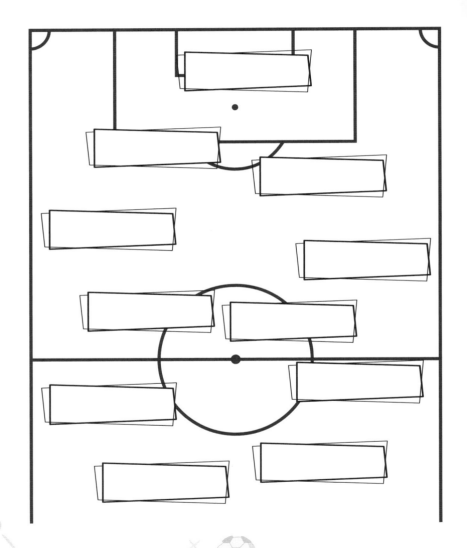

Fill in your ultimate women's XI for England and USA.

USA

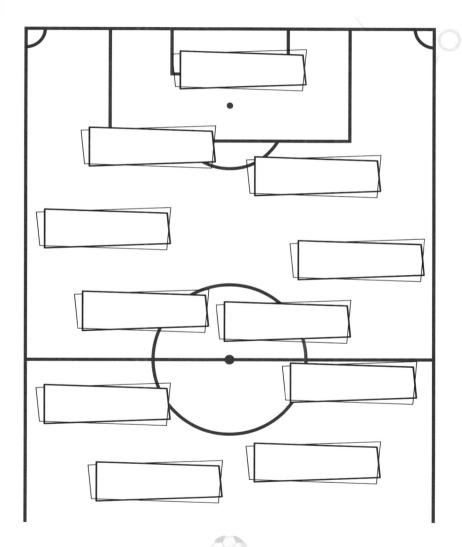

QUIZZES AND PUZZLES

It's time to put your thinking cap on as we test you with a slippery selection of quirky quizzes and puzzling puzzles.

Figuring out these brainteasers is only half the fun though – you'll learn loads about football as you go along!

GOLDEN SHOE WINNERS

The players listed below as anagrams are all winners
of the Golden Shoe – the award given to the top
goal scorer across all of Europe's leagues each season.
Can you unscramble them? We've added the player's year and
club, and the number of letters in their name to help you out!

	Anagram	Year / Club	Answer
	COAL UNIT	2005-6 / Fiorentina 4-4	Luca Toni
1	MR STEVO C BANANA	1985-6 / Ajax 5-3-6	
2	HIP PELVIS LINK	1999-2000 / Sunderland 5-8	
3	OL SHARK SINNER	2000-1 / Celtic 6-7	
4	GOAL OR FINED	2004-5 / Villa Real 5-6	
5	ANTI TESCO CROFT	2006-7 / Roma 9-5	
6	ACTOR RON IS AN IDOL	2007-8 / Man U 9-7	
7	I SMELL NOISE	2009-10 / Barcelona 6-5	
8	I OR MICE LIMBO	2019-20 / Lazio 4-8	

FOOTBALL HISTORY QUIZ

Football's been around for a lot longer than you think, so there's loads of fascinating history to explore. Let's journey back in time, to the dawn of the beautiful game, and test your knowledge with this historical quiz.

1 Which William Shakespeare play from the 1590s mentions a game called 'football'?

A: A Comedy of Errors
B: Hamlet
C: Much Ado About Nothing

2 Founded in November 1862, N_ _ _ _ / C_ _ _ _ _ is the world's oldest League club.

3 Founded in October 1857, S_ _ _ _ _ _ _ D F.C. is the world's oldest football club.

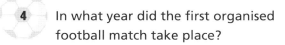

4 In what year did the first organised football match take place?

A: 1852
B: 1863
C: 1870

5 The first-ever international men's football match took place in 1872 between England and...

A: Scotland
B: Germany
C: Brazil

6 And the first-ever women's international took place in 1881 between England and...

A: Brazil
B: Germany
C: Scotland

7 Penalties were first introduced in 1891. What was the original nickname for a penalty?

A: The Kick of Death
B: The Boot of Destiny
C: The Ball of Justice

LET'S CELEBRATE!

You've just scored a worldie and now it's time to celebrate! Will you do a backflip, a little dance or perhaps a knee slide?

Below are a selection of iconic celebrations. Draw a line to match each celebration to its famous footballer.

1

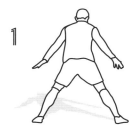

2

3

LUIS
SUÁREZ

KYLIAN
MBAPPÉ

CRISTIANO
RONALDO

PAUL
POGBA

MO
SALAH

GARETH
BALE

4

5

6

BOX TO BOX PLAYER

Warning: this challenge will drive you round the twist! Grab a pen and paper and make as many football-related words as you can from the letters in the boxes.

P	L	O
U	G	S
A	C	F

We reckon there are at least nineteen in the first box and twenty-six in the second. There are one or two player names as well.

Helpful hint: the words you find are football-related. If you find the word 'close', for example, that's okay – TV commentators use it all the time!

S	A	K
R	O	T
E	C	L

WORLD CUP JUMBLE

GERMANY	SWITZERLAND
CHILE	RUSSIA
ARGENTINA	FRANCE
QATAR	ITALY
USA	JAPAN
SWEDEN	MEXICO
URUGUAY	ITALY
FRANCE	BRAZIL
BRAZIL	SPAIN
MEXICO	SOUTH AFRICA
ENGLAND	GERMANY

Can you believe the World Cup is almost 100 years old?
We've mixed up the locations of every final since 1930,
so all you have to do is put them in order. Some finals
have taken place in the same country more than once.
You might need to do a little research to find the answers!

1930 _____

1934 _____

1938 _____

1950 _____

1954 _____

1958 _____

1962 _____

1966 _____

1970 _____

1974 _____

1978 _____

1982 _____

1986 _____

1990 _____

1994 _____

1998 _____

2002 _____

2006 _____

2010 _____

2014 _____

2018 _____

2022 _____

WHO SAID IT?

1. Football is a simple game; 22 men chase a ball for 90 minutes and at the end, the G_ _ _ _ _ s win.

2. Some people think football is a matter of life and death. I assure you it's more i_ _ _ _ _ _ _ t than that.

3. It was the h_ _d of God.

4. It's a f_ _ _ y old game.

These quotes are from some of the best talkers
in the business. All you have to do is match each
quote to the person that said it. Simple, right?
There's just one thing: we've left out a word
in each quote, to make it a little bit harder.

E. HOWARD WILKINSON   **G. IAN RUSH**
F. JIMMY GREAVES   **H. BILL SHANKLY**

5. He's as daft
as a b_ _ _ h.

6. My parents have been there for
me, ever since I was about s_ _ _ n.

7. I couldn't settle in Italy. It was
like living in a f_ _ _ _ _ n country.

8. I'm a firm believer that if you
score one goal the other team
has to score t_o to win.

THE MISSING LETTERS ROUND

J _ M _ E   V _ R _ Y

Leicester City goal machine

P _ R _ I _ K   T _ I _ T _ E

Scottish footie team

J _ R _ AN   H _ N _ E _ S _ N

Liverpool midfield general

G _ L _ T _ S _ R _ Y

Turkish football team

E _ I _ E   S _ I _ H   R _ W _

Arsenal youngster, the 'Croydon De Bruyne'

So, we're about halfway through the Quizzes section and your brain's probably hurting! Time for a slightly easier set of questions – but not too easy. Complete the names of the players and teams below by filling in the missing letters.
G_O_ / L_C_!

W_L_E_H_M_T_N W_N_E_E_S

Midlands club

E_I _S_N C_V_N_

Uruguay striker

S_M_D_R_A

Italian team from Genoa

R_B_R_ L_W_N_O_S_I

Polish-born striker

P_N_T_I_A_K_S

Greek team from Athens

WHO'S IN CHARGE?

Football coaches are known for their cross words – especially when their team's 2–1 down at half time! So, we've created this crossword (see what we did there?) puzzle featuring famous coaches. See if you can fill them all in.

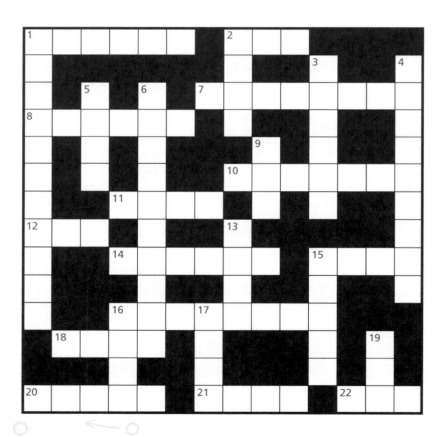

ACROSS CLUES

1 Marcelo. Eccentric Leeds coach (6)

2 Paisley. Liverpool boss in the 70s and 80s (3)

7 The Special One (8)

8 Kevin. Striker and ex-England coach (6)

10 Neil. W_R_O_K (7)

11 Paul, AKA the Guv'nor (4)

12 Ex-Spurs coach Andre Villas-Boas, initially (3)

14 _ _ _ _ _ _ / Edinburgh. Ex-Spurs defender who managed Leyton Orient. (anagram of STUJNI) (6)

15 Former Wimbledon coach Mr Bassett (4)

16 Lee Bowyer and Nigel Adkins have both managed Charlton A_ _ _ _ _ _ C (8)

18 Jimmy. Managed Coventry and presented Match of the Day (4)

20 Avram. Ex-Chelsea boss (5)

21 Garry _ _ _ _ . Managed Swansea and Leeds, among others. Sounds like a holy man (4)

22 World's best coach? Man City fans think so (3)

DOWN CLUES

1 Franz. German. Won the World Cup as captain (1974) and coach (1990) (11)

2 Tony. Managed Man City In the 80s. His name is also what you're reading (4)

3 Zizou (6)

4 Ole Gunnar _ _ _ _ _ _ _ _ _ (9)

5 Smith. Aston Villa coach (4)

6 Ralph. Southampton's Austrian manager (10)

9 Louis _ _ _ Gaal (3)

13 Dennis _ _ _ _. One of Wimbledon's 'Crazy Gang', he also played for Chelsea and managed Leeds and Swindon (4)

15 Sean. Burnley boss (5)

16 _ _ _ _ / Ball: '66 World Cup winner; managed Pompey (4)

17 _ _ _ _ / Brady. Irish Arsenal legend who managed Celtic in the 1990s (anagram of MALI) (4)

19 At Chelsea, strikers (now coaches) Jimmy Floyd Hasselbaink and Eidur Gudjohnsen were 'Fire and _ _ _' (3)

STADIUM NUMBER PUZZLE

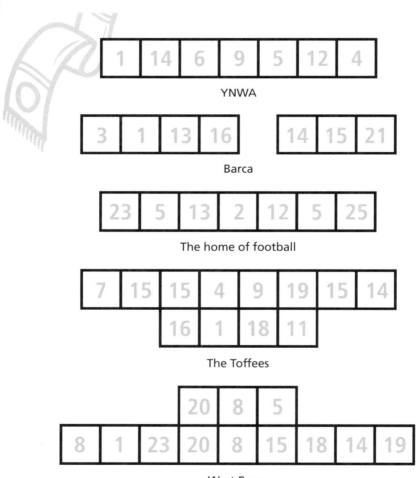

1	14	6	9	5	12	4

YNWA

3	1	13	16

14	15	21

Barca

23	5	13	2	12	5	25

The home of football

7	15	15	4	9	19	15	14

16	1	18	11

The Toffees

20	8	5

8	1	23	20	8	15	18	14	19

West Brom

108

Work out the names of these football arenas
by cracking the code. It looks hard, but once
you get going it's great fun.
To get you started, A=1, B=2, C=3 and so on…

(We've added some clues, too.)

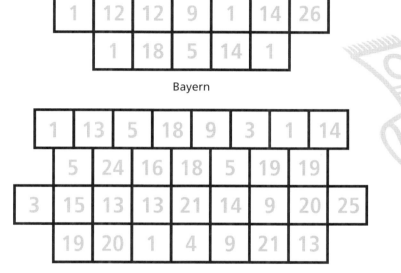

1	12	12	9	1	14	26
	1	18	5	14	1	

Bayern

1	13	5	18	9	3	1	14
	5	24	16	18	5	19	19
3	15	13	13	21	14	9	20	25
	19	20	1	4	9	21	13

The Seagulls

	19	20	
10	1	13	5	19
	16	1	18	11

Haway the Lads!

PICTURE THIS

Some players have names you can paint a picture with, literally. All of the professional players listed here have names that sound like items. We've given you the first one, to get the, er, ball rolling – it's your job to work out the rest.

Alan   ⚽ | Alan Ball

Tim   🌸 | Tim _____

Theo   🧱 + 🎹 | Theo _____

👣 + 🦵   Adams | _____ Adams

😇   Di María | _____ Di María

🐦 🚚   Persie | _____ ___ Persie

Harry   👁 👁 | Harry _____

THE LANGUAGE OF FOOTBALL

Match up the term for 'football' below with the correct language. We've added a couple of clues and we've given you the first answer for free!

Croatia	**Fussball (lots of World Cup wins!)**
Czech	Calcio (Mamma mia!)
Danish	**Jalgpall (anagram of 'antinose')**
Dutch	Podósfairo (kebabs, moussaka)
Estonian	**Ball-coise (bagpipes)**
Finnish	Pêl-droed (the red dragon)
German	**Fotbal (capital city: Prague)**
Greek	Peil (the Emerald Isle)
Icelandic	**Fudbal (capital city: Belgrade)**
Irish	Jalkapallo (capital city: Helsinki)
Italian	**Voetbal (all in orange)**
Polish	Fotboll (Zlatan!)
Scottish	**Nogomet (Luka Modrić)**
Serbian	Fótbolti (knocked England out of 2016 Euros)
Spanish	**Piłka nożna (capital city: Warsaw)**
Swedish	Fútbol (Tiki-taka)
Welsh	**Fodbold (Scandinavian pastry)**

DO YOU KNOW YOUR EUROS?

1 For the 2020 Euros, how many Harrys played for England during qualification? Name them.

2 Sokratis Papastathopoulos and Wojciech Szczęsny were sent off in a 2012 Euros match between Greece and Poland. Which English club did both men play for (though not at the same time)?

3 In 2016 Taulant Xhaka (Albania) and Granit Xhaka (Switzerland) became the first brothers to play against each other in the Euros.

TRUE or FALSE?

England hasn't won the Euros – yet – but they live in hope. While you wait, why not kill some time tackling this Euros-themed quiz?

4 Cristiano Ronaldo is the Euros finals top scorer (nine goals), along with which 1980s French legend?

A: Michel Platini   **C:** Jean Tigana
B: Alain Giresse

5 What was unique about the 2000 Euros final, won by France?

A: Six players were sent off
B: The referee quit at half time
C: It was decided by a Golden Goal

6 Martin Ødegaard made his international debut in a Euros qualifier in 2016, aged just 15 years and 300 days, for which country?

RECORD BREAKERS

We all love a stat, and these are the best of the best.
Do you know football's oldest, youngest, tallest
and smallest players? Work out all this and
more in our record-breakers puzzle.

1 Ezzeldin Bahader of Egypt became the world's oldest
player in 2020, taking to the field at the age of...

A: 56 years and 253 days   **C:** 74 years and 125 days
B: 61 years and 40 days

2 On 19 July 2009, Mauricio Baldivieso made
his professional debut in Bolivia aged...

A: 12 years and 362 days   **C:** 15 years and 61 days
B: 14 years and 174 days

3 Simon Bloch Jørgensen from Denmark is the world's
tallest professional footballer, standing at...

A: 2.05m (6ft 7in)   **C:** 2.15m (7ft)
B: 2.10m (6ft 9in)

4 Brazil's Élton José Xavier Gomes and Argentina's Daniel Alberto Villalva Barrios are jointly the world's shortest players, at …

A: 1.54m (5ft 0.6in)   **C:** 1.60m (5ft 2.4in)
B: 1.57m (5ft 1.5in)

5 As of 2021, Wycombe Wanderers' striker Adebayo Akinfenwa was the world's heaviest player, at a scales-busting…

A: 100kg (15st 11lb)   **C:** 106kg (16st 7lb)
B: 102kg (16st 1lb)

6 The leading goalscorer of all time is…

A: Pelé   **C:** Or… someone else
B: Cristiano Ronaldo

7 Former England goalie Peter Shilton holds which enviable world record?

A: Most clean sheets   **C:** Curliest perm ever
B: Most games played

FIND THE FOOTBALLER

Hidden in the grid below are the names of sixteen famous footballers. Think you can find them all? We've given you Joe Hart to get you started – the names read up to down as well as from left to right.

T	O	H	Z	E	B	R	O	N	A	L	D	I	N	H	O
A	M	A	L	G	O	X	F	L	E	L	C	H	S	O	N
S	E	R	G	I	O	R	A	M	O	S	T	Y	L	Q	G
A	S	R	U	P	M	S	O	C	R	A	T	E	S	U	O
D	R	Y	S	E	L	H	U	R	S	C	R	U	B	U	L
I	S	K	Y	L	I	A	N	M	B	A	P	P	E	T	O
O	H	A	Z	G	O	F	F	L	Y	B	A	S	T	I	K
M	I	N	I	S	N	U	G	G	R	T	I	M	H	Y	A
A	Z	E	J	O	E	H	A	R	T	H	R	A	M	E	N
N	A	C	K	Y	L	E	W	A	L	K	E	R	E	N	T
E	G	D	Y	S	M	M	P	L	Y	K	U	T	A	Z	E
A	R	P	L	N	E	T	F	L	I	C	H	A	D	L	E
V	E	E	R	O	S	A	M	K	E	R	R	Y	I	M	P
I	A	L	O	S	S	I	S	S	U	K	I	S	C	O	S
P	L	E	Z	Z	I	C	O	D	I	F	C	O	O	R	W

KYLIAN MBAPPE	SERGIO RAMOS	MARTA	RONALDINHO
HARRY KANE	ZICO	BETH MEAD	PELE
LIONEL MESSI	NGOLO KANTE	SAM KERR	ISCO
KYLE WALKER	JOE HART	SADIO MANE	SOCRATES

BADGE OF HONOUR

Each football team has a club crest, and some are more recognisable than others. Do you think you can name the team just by looking at the silhouette?

1.

2.

3.

4.

5.

6.

7.

8.

THE FA CUP

The FA Cup is the greatest club tournament there is. It's got everything: history, glory, giant-killings, cup upsets, great goals and amazing stories.

Let's see how much you know about it.

1 When was the first FA Cup final: 1867, 1872 or 1881?

2 And where was it held?

A: Wembley   **C:** Windsor Great
B: The Oval   Park

3 The largest attendance for an FA Cup final, in 1923, was more than 120,000.

TRUE or FALSE?

4 How many times has Arsenal won the FA Cup: 12, 13 or 14?

5 Which team has been in the most FA Cup finals (so far) without winning?

A: Leicester   **C:** Newcastle

B: Burnley

6 The highest-scoring FA Cup tie took place in 1887, between Preston and Hyde. The score was:

A: 9–3   **B:** 14–11   **C:** 26–0

7 Only one non-English club has won the FA Cup. Can you guess who?

8 In 1985, Manchester United's Kevin Moran achieved which infamous 'honour' in an FA Cup final?

A: First substitute to be substituted

B: First player to miss a penalty kick

C: First player to be sent off

WORLD CUP
NAME GAME

FRANCE

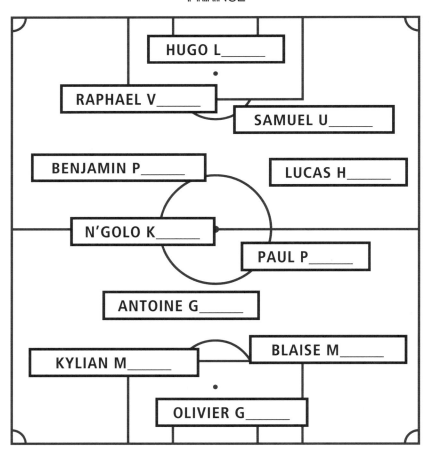

HUGO L_____

RAPHAEL V_____

SAMUEL U_____

BENJAMIN P_____

LUCAS H_____

N'GOLO K_____

PAUL P_____

ANTOINE G_____

BLAISE M_____

KYLIAN M_____

OLIVIER G_____

The 2018 World Cup semi-final between France and Belgium was one of the most star-studded games of recent times.

We've given you the first names of every player — all you have to do is fill in their famous surnames!

BELGIUM

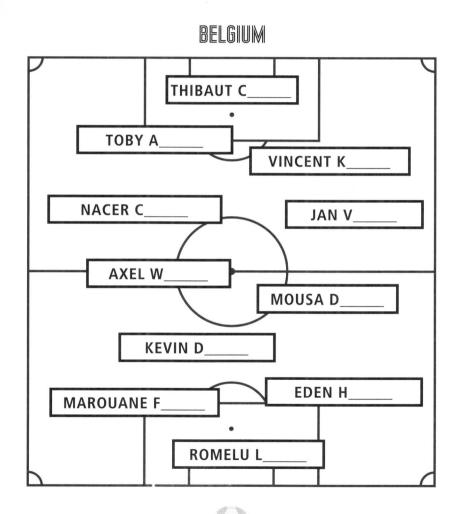

THIBAUT C_____

TOBY A_____

VINCENT K_____

NACER C_____

JAN V_____

AXEL W_____

MOUSA D_____

KEVIN D_____

MAROUANE F_____

EDEN H_____

ROMELU L_____

CHAMPIONS LEAGUE QUIZ

It was once the European Cup and now it's the Champions League. Whatever you call it, everyone wants to win the most prestigious club competition in the world.

Shall we find out what you know about it?

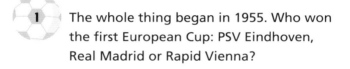

1 The whole thing began in 1955. Who won the first European Cup: PSV Eindhoven, Real Madrid or Rapid Vienna?

2 In the 65 years from 1955 to 2020, how many different clubs have won the tournament?

A: 22
B: 33
C: 44

3 Six clubs from the UK have won the European Cup/Champions League up to 2020. How many can you name?

A: D:

B: E:

C: F:

4 Only one player has lifted the Champions League trophy with three different clubs – Ajax, Real Madrid and Milan:

C_ _ _ _ _ _E / S_ _ _ _ _ F (he's Dutch).

5 Two players have scored 8 hat-tricks in the Champions League – you can probably guess who...

6 Which Barcelona player became the youngest ever Champions League goal scorer in 2019? His name's an anagram of USAN / FIAT

ONE NAME LEADS TO ANOTHER

Have you noticed how some people's surnames can also be
used to complete other names or phrases?
For example, Alan Ball and Ball Boy.
Work out these footballers' surnames from our silly clues.

DECLAN | R | | | E | PUDDING

STUART | D | | | | S | COWBOYS

MATTY | C | | | H | CONVERTERS

MASON | M | | | | T | EVEREST

JAMES | J | | | | N | TIMBERLAKE

HELDER | C | | | A | COFFEE

ALEX | M | | | | N | SCHNEIDERLIN

CHARLIE | A | | M | AND EVE

THOMAS	M _ _ _ _ R	YOGHURT
THOMAS	P _ _ _ _ Y	LIKE IT'S 1999
WAYNE	B _ _ _ _ E	OVER TROUBLED WATER
ROB	H _ _ _ _ _ G	OUT FOR A HERO
WILL	F _ _ _ Y	'CROSS THE MERSEY
KEVIN	L _ _ G	JOHN SILVER
EDEN	H _ _ _ _ D	WARNING LIGHTS
JILL	S _ _ _ T	OF THE ANTARCTIC
BETH	E _ _ _ _ _ D	LOSE TO GERMANY ON PENALTIES
EMILE SMITH	R _ _ E	ROW ROW YOUR BOAT
DELE	A _ _ I	BABA AND THE FORTY THIEVES

GOLDEN BOOT
GOLDEN BOYS

This crossword puzzle is all about Premier League
Golden Boot winners – who they are, who they play for
and a couple of quirky facts you maybe didn't know.

ACROSS CLUES

6 Ex-Arsenal striker with va-va-voom (7,5)

8 Mr Sutton (5)

9 What the newspapers called 9 Down (4)

11 Leicester goal machine Jamie (5)

12 Dwight _ _ _ _ _. Man U and Trinidad & Tobago (5)

14 6 Across and 13 Down's country (6)

15 All-time leading Premier League scorer (7)

17 Mr Dublin, now a TV presenter and expert (4)

18 Teddy _ _ _ _ingham. Boot winner in 1993 (4)

20 Sergio Agüero's nickname (3)

21 What 2 Down's friends call him (2)

22 Carlos _ _ _ _ _. Anagram of VEETZ (5)

DOWN CLUES

1 Arsenal 2019 Golden Boot winner's initials (1,1,1)

2 Mohamed Salah's nickname is Egypt's M_ _ _ _ (5)

3 Cristiano Ronaldo's brand (3)

4 15 Across is from Newcastle, in the county of Tyne & _ _ _ _ (4)

5 Luis Suárez's homeland (7)

7 Spurs and England captain (5,4)

9 Ex-Chelsea and Ivory Coast striker's first name.
Anagram of RIDEDI (6)

10 Mohamed Salah's country (5)

11 Robin. Arsenal, Man Utd, Holland (3, 6)

13 Nicolas. Arsenal, then Real Madrid (6)

15 Liverpool's 'Mane' man (5)

16 How many times Dimitar Berbatov won the Golden Boot (4)

19 8 Across's middle name: _ _ _ of the Rovers? (3)

STADIUM WORD SEARCH

We had so much fun with the last word search that we've made you another one! This one's all about football equipment – all the bits and bobs you'll need to play the game. There are sixteen items to find!

G	O	A	L	P	O	S	T	S	H	I	R	S	P	Y	L
L	F	L	A	I	S	H	A	W	I	S	H	C	O	R	E
I	F	O	D	T	K	I	T	Z	D	E	V	A	R	U	P
T	S	U	U	E	R	N	E	Q	U	W	U	R	M	N	R
S	E	A	G	T	I	P	Z	E	M	A	N	D	R	I	C
C	F	O	O	T	B	A	L	L	O	T	Y	S	H	O	O
O	Y	N	U	H	A	D	R	O	S	C	Y	Q	U	Z	R
R	N	B	T	G	L	S	O	C	R	H	B	U	G	U	N
E	E	A	F	R	A	N	C	K	R	A	D	Z	N	Z	E
B	Z	L	Y	S	P	O	R	E	F	E	R	E	E	D	R
O	Z	L	N	O	P	S	T	R	A	G	H	D	T	F	F
A	L	B	A	L	K	I	C	H	R	J	I	A	S	E	L
R	U	O	S	M	A	G	I	C	S	P	R	A	Y	N	A
D	B	Y	S	A	P	L	O	W	E	D	R	N	I	N	G
T	A	S	O	W	H	I	S	T	L	E	Y	Y	E	T	S

FOOTBALL	GOALPOSTS	BALLBOYS	VAR
LOCKER	NETS	SCOREBOARD	MAGIC SPRAY
SHINPADS	CORNER FLAG	WHISTLE	WATCH
KIT	REFEREE	CARDS	DUGOUT

THE A TO Z OF THE QATAR WORLD CUP

The Qatar World Cup will be a tournament
like no other: the first one staged in the
Middle East and the only one played in winter.

This A to Z tells you all you need
to know about the country and
the teams hoping to take part.

Your A to Z crash-course introduction to the 2022 World Cup in Qatar starts here: twenty-six facts, figures and amazing bits of info for you to work out.

A Angola and Algeria are two teams attempting to qualify for the finals from which continent, which also begins with 'A'?

B They are ranked number 1 in the world, they reached the World Cup semi-finals last time around, and they are known as the Red Devils. Who are they?

C This country (or a tiny bit of it in the north) is the closest to the North Pole of any nation in World Cup qualification – at 83° 07'N, to be exact.

D He managed France to World Cup glory in 2018 and he'll be trying to do it again in 2022. He is: D_ D_E_ / D_S_H_M_S.

E 'E' is for eleven – the number of teams attempting to qualify from this region, whose teams include Paraguay and Peru. Name the region.

F FIFA is football's governing body, and oversees the World Cup. But what does FIFA stand for? Careful: it's in French!

G What is sculptor Silvio Gazzaniga's claim to World Cup fame? (Clue: this was in 1974, after Brazil won the tournament for the third time in 1970.)

H 'H' is for 'hospitality'. At the Qatar World Cup, how much will a hospitality suite of forty seats cost for the final: £80,000, £250,000 or £1.9 million?

I Gianni I_ _ _ _ _ _ _O is the big boss of FIFA and is in charge of the World Cup. His Italian name means 'little baby' in English!

J 'J' stands for J_ _ _ S Rimet, the French FIFA official who 'invented' the World Cup in 1930.

K This Asian team has no vowels in its name. It is: K _ _ _ _ _ Republic (rearrange these letters to get the answer: KYYZGR).

L The 2022 final will be held at the newly-built Lusail Iconic Stadium. But which traditional Arabic object is it designed to look like: an oud (a stringed instrument), a desert tribesman's headscarf or a woven bowl?

M This country didn't exist until 2006. It's in southeast Europe, and in English its name means 'Black Mountain'.

N This small African country is officially the poorest nation in qualification.

O 'O' stands for 'over-budget'. The 2014 World Cup cost $15 billion and the 2018 tournament cost $11.6 billion. How much is Qatar 2022 expected to cost: $22 billion, $110 billion or $220 billion?

P This country in Central America lost 6–1 to England in 2018, in a very ill-tempered match. It has both a hat and a canal named after it.

Q 'Q' is for Qatar! It's the smallest nation to ever host a World Cup – it's about half the size of Wales. What's that in square kilometres: 11,000, 17,000 or 25,000?

R He will be thirty-seven by the time the 2022 World Cup begins, but (if his country qualifies) it's unthinkable he won't be there. He is, of course, Cristiano R_ _ _ _ _ _ .

S   This tiny European nation is the lowest-ranked team in the world (210th!). They are in England's qualification group and they have never won a competitive game of football.

T   'T' is for temperature. The 2022 World Cup is being held in November/December because Qatar is too hot in the summer. How hot, on average: 33°C, 36°C or 40°C?

U   Which country won the first-ever World Cup in 1930, and again in 1950 – but, despite the best efforts of Luis Suárez and Edinson Cavani, hasn't managed it since?

V   Can you name these four teams in qualification whose names begin with the letter 'V'?

V_ R _ I _ / I_ L _ N _ S

V_ E _ N _ M

V_ N _Z E _A

V_ N _A _U

W Only one country trying to qualify for Qatar 2022 begins with this letter. No clues, it's too easy!

X He's a Swiss midfielder hoping to see his team through to the 2022 finals. He's not Shakira, he's X _ _ _ _ _ N Shaqiri.

Y This Arabic country hopes it will qualify for 2022 as it's virtually next door to Qatar.

Z Which two African nations whose names begin with this letter will be trying to qualify for Qatar 2022? They are anagrams of ZIBAAM and ZEBBWAMI.

ANSWERS

It's time to see how you've done. Hope you're not kicking yourself too many times after reading these solutions!

PAGE 10: BRAINTEASERS
1. He kicks the ball straight up in the air!
2. Simple. The score is always 0-0 before the match kicks off.
3. The fence.
4. The Coach was the goalkeeper's mother.
5. All of them. The crossbar can't jump!
6. Won: 2–1, Drew: 1–1, Lost: 1–2.

PAGE 12: FOOTBALL TRIVIA
1. A. That's a proper pair of flippers!
2. A. Players said the grey made it hard to pick out teammates on the other side of the pitch.
3. C. Look it up on the internet. It's hilarious!
4. A. The Barca star's IQ is 170 (10 points higher than Einstein). Lampard (150) is second highest, and Balotelli (147) is third!

PAGE 16: LOST IN TRANSLATION
Spanish
Una Chilena (A bicycle kick).
    Literally: 'A Chilean' (no idea why!).
Gol Olimpico (Goal scored directly from a corner). Literally: 'Olympic goal'
Arbitro, la hora (Come on ref, blow up).
    Literally: 'Referee, it's time'
Da en el palo (It's hit the post!)
    Literally: 'It's hit the stick'
German
Hexenkessel (An unfriendly crowd).
    Literally: 'the Witches' cauldron'
Sechspunktespiel (It's a six-pointer).
    Literally: 'A six-point game'
Fahrstuhlmannschaft (A yo-yo club).
    Literally: 'An elevator team'
Traumtor (A worldie!).
    Literally: 'Dream goal'
Italian
Lui fa un colpo di testa (He's headed the ball).
    Literally: 'He's made a blow to the head'

Lui fa in Cucchiaio (He's scored a 'Panenka' penalty kick). Literally: 'He's made a spoon'

Lui fa una papera (He's dropped a clanger). Literally: 'He's made a duck' (of the quack quack kind)

Lui fa un tunnel (He's nutmegged him!) Literally: 'He's made a tunnel'

French

Il est aveugle ou quoi (Is the ref blind?). Literally: 'Is he blind or what?'

Une courte victoire (A narrow win). Literally: 'A narrow victory'

Aux chiottes l'arbitre (This ref's rubbish). Literally: 'Put the ref in the toilet'

Passe la balle, nom de dieu (Pass it, now!). Literally: 'Pass the ball, in the name of God!'

PAGE 20: FUNNY FOOTBALL STORIES
They're all true!

PAGE 22: TAKE THE STRING CHALLENGE
Player B has lifted the cup!

PAGE 24: HOME TURF

Manchester United	Old Trafford
Leicester City	King Power Stadium
Club América	Aztec Stadium
Arsenal	Emirates Stadium
Leeds United	Elland Road
Hull City	KCOM Stadium
Portsmouth F.C.	Fratton Park
Watford F.C.	Vicarage Road
Liverpool	Anfield
Manchester City	Etihad Stadium
Blackburn Rovers	Ewood Park
AFC Wimbledon	Plough Lane
Borussia Dortmund	Signal Iduna Park
A.C. Milan	San Siro
Real Madrid	Santiago Bernabéu
Barcelona	Camp Nou
Juventus	Allianz Stadium
AFC Ajax	Johan Cruijff ArenA
Palermo	Stadio Renzo Barbera
AS Monaco	Stade Louis II
PSG	Le Parc des Princes

PAGE 26: JOIN THE DOTS

PAGE 44: PIN THE INJURY ON THE PLAYER
1: C (Dislocated glenoid)
2. G (Pulled hamstring)
3. J (Damaged Achilles)
4. B (Fractured clavicle)
5. A (Concussion)
6. H (Quadriceps strain)
7. E (ACL)
8. I (Shin splints)
9. D (Sprained impingement)
10. K (Broken metatarsal)
11. F (Groin pull)

PAGE 48: JACK THE LADS
1. Jack BUTLAND   2. Jack CHARLTON
3. Jack O'CONNELL   4. Jack ROBINSON
5. Jack STEPHENS   6. Jack RODWELL
7. Jack JENKINS   8. Jack CORK
9. Jack HARRISON   10. Jack GREALISH
11. Jack WILSHERE

PAGE 51: WHERE IN THE WORLD

PAGE 52: The UK
1. E: London   2. C: Glasgow
3. F: Manchester   4. A: Ipswich
5. D: Newcastle (or Newcastle upon Tyne)
6. B: Cardiff

PAGE 54: France

1. D: Paris
2. C: Monaco
3. B: Lens
4. E: Dijon
5. A: Marseille

PAGE 56: Italy

1. E: Naples
2. B: Rome
3. F: Milan
4. A: Palermo
5. C: Bari
6. D: Pisa

PAGE 58: Spain and Portugal

1. C: Barcelona
2. E: Madrid
3. A: Lisbon
4. F: Seville
5. B: Porto
6. D: Malaga

PAGE 60: Germany

1. E: Munich
2. F: Mönchengladbach
3. A: Frankfurt
4. B: Hamburg
5. D: Berlin
6. C: Bremen

PAGE 62: USA

1. E: Washington D.C.
2. A: New York City
3. F: Los Angeles
4. C: Houston
5. B: Miami
6. D: Nashville

PAGE 64: South America

1. C: Buenos Aires
2. A: São Paulo
3. D: Rio de Janeiro
4. E: Bogotá
5. B: Cerro de Pasco

PAGE 66: Africa

1. D: Cairo
2. C: Nairobi
3. E: Harare
4. B: Cape Town
5. A: Kinshasa

PAGE 68: YOU'RE THE REF

1. b) Yellow card the player and restart play. Taking off your top is a bookable offence whether you score or not. After all, who wants to see a footballer's hairy chest!

2. c) Make the player retake the pen: the keeper must be on the line for a spot kick, not behind or in front of it.

3. c) Yellow or red card the manager: if it's a bookable offence, someone has to be punished. If you don't know who, the manager/head coach has to take the hit.

4. b) Red card the player and award a penalty: yep, he's off (Luis Suárez once did this in the World Cup for Uruguay against Ghana. Naughty boy!)

5. c) Give a direct free kick. He's committed an offence, but not a major one worthy of a pen.

6. b) Indirect free kick to the defending team. The attacking team has committed a minor offence, with no contact made on an opposing player.

7. a) Goal kick (i.e. disallow the goal). The ball has to touch at least two players after a drop ball to be considered properly back in play. Weird, huh?

8. c) Give a penalty with no card. It's a foul in the box, so definitely a pen, but as there's no intent you don't need to book the defender.

9. a) One. A team must have seven players for the game to continue.

10. b) Indirect free kick. Like answer 6, it's a minor offence, with no player-to-player contact.

11. a) Allow the goal. You can't be offside from a throw-in. No one knows why – you just can't!

12. b) No: you've not officially waved him on yet. He has to first enter the field of play to be an active player. Then he can go back off and take the throw-in. Mad, eh?

13. a) Corner kick to the defending team. This is a crazy one: play goes up the other end of the pitch and the team that was just defending a corner now gets to take a corner themselves!

14. c) Provide medical treatment for any injured players. Unless you're a doctor, of course, in which case you can help out unofficially.

15. b) No, the goal was scored after you intended to blow the whistle. Seems

unfair, doesn't it? But the ref is the sole timekeeper in a match, and if they decide the game is over, it's over – whether they blow the whistle or not.

16.b) Give a goal kick to the defending team. You can't throw the ball directly into the net (unless you're a goalkeeper, in which case it's OK – but very embarrassing!).

PAGE 94: QUIZZES AND PUZZLES

PAGE 95: GOLDEN SHOE WINNERS
1. Marco Van Basten
2. Kevin Phillips
3. Henrik Larsson
4. Diego Forlan
5. Francesco Totti
6. Cristiano Ronaldo
7. Lionel Messi
8. Ciro Immobile

PAGE 96: FOOTBALL HISTORY QUIZ
1. A. Appropriately enough!
2. Notts County
3. Sheffield F.C. – but who did they play against?
4. B. Between Barnes F.C. and Richmond F.C. in London. It ended 0–0.
5. A. And the score was… 0–0!
6. C. Scotland won 3–0!
7. A. Sounds painful.

PAGE 98: LET'S CELEBRATE
1. Cristiano Ronaldo
2. Mo Salah
3. Gareth Bale
4. Kyllian Mbappé
5. Paul Pogba
6. Luis Suárez

PAGE 99: BOX TO BOX PLAYER
Box 1. We found:
ALF (as in Alf Ramsey), FLAG, FLAGS, GOAL, GOALS, FOUL, FOULS, CUP, CUPS, FA CUP, FA CUPS, CAP, CAPS, SLOG, SLAP, FLAP, FLAPS, SCALP, CAFU (Brazil player)
Box 2. We found:
SOCK, LOCKER, SCORE, ROCKET, CLOSE, CLOSER, LOSE, LOSER, LOST, SACK, TACKLE, TACKLES, TACKLER, RACE, ROAST, SLACK, TRACK, TEA (half-time drink), TALK, LATE,

RATE, STROKE, CLEAR, ASTRO (as in astro turf), (Diego) COSTA, (Martin) SKRTEL

PAGE 100: WORLD CUP JUMBLE
1930 Uruguay	1934 Italy
1938 France	1950 Brazil
1954 Switzerland	1958 Sweden
1962 Chile	1966 England
1970 Mexico	1974 Germany
1978 Argentina	1982 Spain
1986 Mexico	1990 Italy
1994 USA	1998 France
2002 Japan	2006 Germany
2010 South Africa	2014 Brazil
2018 Russia	2022 Qatar

PAGE 102: WHO SAID IT?
1. D, former England striker. (Missing word: Germans).
2. H, Liverpool manager 1959-74. (Missing word: important).
3. A, handballed a goal in the 1986 World Cup. (Missing word: hand).
4. F, England striker of the 1960s. (Missing word: funny).
5. B, former England manager. (Missing word: brush).
6. C. (Missing word: seven).
7. G. (Missing word: foreign).
8. E, ex-Leeds manager. (Missing word: two).

PAGE 104: THE MISSING LETTERS ROUND
1. Jamie Vardy
2. Partick Thistle
3. Jordan Henderson
4. Galatasaray
5. Emile Smith Rowe
6. Wolverhampton Wanderers
7. Edinson Cavani
8. Sampdoria
9. Robert Lewandowski
10.Panathinaikos

PAGE 106: WHO'S IN CHARGE?

Crossword grid:
- B I E L S A / B O B
- E / O / Z / S
- C / D H M O U R I N H O
- K E E G A N / K / D / L
- E / A S / V / A / S
- N N E / W A R N O C K
- B / I N C E / N / E / J
- A V B H / W / E / A
- U / J U S T I N / D A V E
- E / T / S / Y / R
- R / A T H L E T I C
- H I L L / I / H / I
- A / A / E / C
- G R A N T M O N K P E P

PAGE 108: STADIUM NUMBER PUZZLE

A. Anfield
B. Camp Nou
C. Wembley
D. Goodison Park
E. The Hawthorns
F. Allianz Arena
G. American Express Community Stadium
H. St James' Park

PAGE 110: PICTURE THIS

Alan Ball
Theo Walcott
Ángel di María
Harry Winks

Tim Flowers
Tony Adams
Robin van Persie

PAGE 111: THE LANGUAGE OF FOOTBALL

Croatia	Nogomet
Czech	Fotbal
Danish	Fodbold
Dutch	Voetbal
Estonian	Jalgpall
Finnish	Jalkapallo
German	Fussball
Greek	Podósfairo
Icelandic	Fótbolti
Irish	Peil
Italian	Calcio
Polish	Piłka nozna
Scottish	Ball-coise
Serbian	Fudbal
Spanish	Fútbol
Swedish	Fotboll
Welsh	Pêl-droed

PAGE 112: DO YOU KNOW YOUR EUROS?

1. Three: Harry Kane, Harry McGuire, Harry Winks
2. Arsenal
3. True. The Swiss won 1-0.
4. A.
5. C. Scored by David Trezeguet
6. Norway

PAGE 114: RECORD BREAKERS

1. C. Really!
2. A.
3. B. He's a goalkeeper, of course.
4. A. Small, but perfectly formed.
5. B. Imagine him coming at you!
6. C. Czechoslovakia's Josef Bican, who played from 1931-56 and banged in more than 800 goals.
7. B. He played 1,390 games for clubs and country.

PAGE 116: FIND THE FOOTBALLER

T	O	N	Z	E	B	R	O	N	A	L	D	I	N	H	O
A	M	A	L	G	O	X	F	L	E	L	C	H	S	O	N
S	E	R	G	I	O	R	A	M	O	S	T	Y	L	Q	G
A	S	R	U	P	M	S	O	C	R	A	T	E	S	U	O
D	R	Y	S	E	L	H	U	R	S	C	R	U	B	U	L
I	S	K	Y	L	I	A	N	M	B	A	P	P	E	T	O
O	H	A	Z	G	O	F	F	L	Y	B	A	S	T	I	K
M	I	N	I	S	N	U	G	G	R	T	I	M	H	Y	A
A	Z	E	J	O	E	H	A	R	T	H	R	A	M	E	N
N	A	C	K	Y	E	W	A	L	K	E	R	E	N	T	
E	G	D	Y	S	M	M	P	L	Y	K	U	T	A	Z	E
A	R	P	L	N	E	T	F	L	I	C	H	A	D	L	E
V	E	E	R	O	S	A	M	K	E	R	R	Y	I	M	P
I	A	L	O	S	S	I	S	S	U	K	I	S	C	O	S
P	L	E	Z	Z	I	C	O	D	I	F	C	O	O	R	W

PAGE 117: BADGE OF HONOUR
1. Manchester United 2. Barcelona
3. Liverpool   4. PSG
5. Bayern Munich   6. Real Madrid
7. Benfica   8. A.C. Milan

PAGE 118: THE FA CUP
1. 1872 – Wanderers 0–1 Royal Engineers.
2. B. It's just not cricket!
3. True. No one knows the exact number, but it's thought be more than 300,000! (Bolton beat West Ham 2–0).
4. 14 – more than anyone else.
5. A. Leicester – 4 times.
6. C. 26–0 to Preston. A bit one-sided, ey?
7. Cardiff City, in 1927.
8. C.

PAGE 120: WORLD CUP NAME GAME
France

Hugo Lloris	Benjamin Pavard
Raphaël Varane	Samuel Umtiti
Lucas Hernandez	N'Golo Kanté
Paul Pogba	Kylian Mbappé
Antoine Griezmann	Blaise Matuidi
Olivier Giroud	

Belgium

Thibaut Courtois	Jan Vertonghen
Vincent Kompany	Toby Alderweireld
Nacer Chadli	Mousa Dembélé
Axel Witsel	Eden Hazard
Marouane Fellaini	Kevin De Bruyne
Romelu Lukaku	

PAGE 122: CHAMPIONS LEAGUE QUIZ
1. Real Madrid (they always win), 4–3 against Stade de Reims.
2. A: 22. Yes, we were surprised it's so few.
3. Celtic (1967), Liverpool (1977, 1978, 1981, 1984, 2005, 2019), Manchester United (1968, 1999, 2008), Nottingham Forest (1979, 1980), Aston Villa (1982), Chelsea (2012).
4. Clarence Seedorf.
5. Lionel Messi and Cristiano Ronaldo, of course.
6. Ansu Fati.

PAGE 124: ONE NAME LEADS TO ANOTHER
Declan RICE Pudding
Stuart DALLAS Cowboys
Matty CASH Converters
Mason MOUNT Everest
James JUSTIN Timberlake
Helder COSTA Coffee
Alex MORGAN Schneiderlin
Charlie ADAM and Eve
Thomas MULLER Yogurt
Thomas PARTEY Like it's 1999
Wayne BRIDGE Over Troubled Water
Rob HOLDING Out For a Hero
Will FERRY 'Cross The Mersey
Kevin LONG John Silver
Eden HAZARD Warning Lights
Jill SCOTT of the Antarctic
Beth ENGLAND Lose to Germany on penalties.
Emile Smith ROWE Row Row Your Boat.
Dele ALLI Baba and the Forty Thieves

PAGE 126: GOLDEN BOOT GOLDEN BOYS

PAGE 128: STADIUM WORD SEARCH

G	O	A	L	P	O	S	T	S	H	I	R	S	P	Y	L
L	F	L	A	I	S	H	A	W	I	S	H	C	O	R	E
I	F	O	D	T	K	I	T	Z	D	E	V	A	R	U	P
T	S	U	U	E	R	N	E	Q	U	W	U	R	M	N	R
S	E	A	G	T	I	P	Z	E	M	A	N	D	R	I	C
C	F	O	O	T	B	A	L	L	O	T	Y	S	H	O	O
O	Y	N	U	H	A	D	R	O	S	C	Y	Q	U	Z	R
R	N	B	T	G	L	S	O	C	R	H	B	U	G	U	N
E	E	A	F	R	A	N	C	K	R	A	D	Z	N	Z	E
B	Z	L	Y	S	P	O	R	E	F	E	R	E	E	D	R
O	Z	L	N	O	P	S	T	R	A	G	H	D	T	F	F
A	L	B	A	L	K	I	C	H	R	J	I	A	S	E	L
R	U	O	S	M	A	G	I	C	S	P	R	A	Y	N	A
D	B	Y	S	A	P	L	O	W	E	D	R	N	I	N	G
T	A	S	O	W	H	I	S	T	L	E	Y	Y	E	T	S

PAGE 129: **THE A TO Z OF THE QATAR WORLD CUP**

A. Africa. 54 teams from Africa are attempting to qualify.

B. Belgium.

C. Canada, at Cape Columbia, Ellesmere Island, Nunavut.

D. Didier Deschamps. He won it as a player in 1998, too.

E. South America.

F. Federation Internationale de Football Association.

G. He designed the new World Cup trophy, after Brazil was allowed to keep the old one.

H. £1.9 million! You get free drinks and snacks though.

I. Gianni Infantino.

J. Jules Rimet – and the trophy was named after him until 1970.

K. It's Kyrgyz Republic.

L. A woven bowl.

M. Montenegro.

N. Niger.

O. $220 billion. Yep, that's $220 billion. It does include building a whole new city, called Lusail, though.

P. Panama.

Q. 11,000 sq km. You can drive from one end of it to the other in two hours, and all the stadiums are no further than 55km apart. It will be possible to watch three games in three different stadiums in one day!

R. Ronaldo.

S. San Marino.

T. 40°C. Your ice cream won't last long in that!

U. Uruguay.

V. Virgin Islands, Vietnam, Venezuela, Vanuatu.

W. Wales!

X. Xherdan Shaqiri.

Y. Yemen.

Z. Zambia and Zimbabwe.

CAN'T GET ENOUGH OF
ULTIMATE FOOTBALL HEROES?

**Check out heroesfootball.com
for quizzes, games, and competitions!**

**Plus join the Ultimate Football Heroes
Fan Club to score exclusive content
and be the first to hear about new
books and events.
heroesfootball.com/subscribe/**